WILSON

MW00658688

The Country of Spirit

SELECTED WRITINGS

J. Appleseed & Co.
San Francisco and Boston

ISBN 0-9626795-2-6

Editor: James F. Lawrence
Book design and typesetting: Dana Design, Mountain View, CA
Cover design: dba Design and Illustration, San Carlos, CA

Typeset in Goudy with Korinna accents.
Manufactured in the United States of America.

"A Mystic Looks at Swedenborg" was first published in *Emanuel Swedenborg: A Continuing Vision*, Robin Larsen, General Editor, Swedenborg Foundation, New York City, 1988.

"The Mystery of Ordinary Experiencing" was first published as a chapter in *The Natural Depth in Man*, by Wilson Van Dusen, Harper and Row, San Francisco, 1972.

"Reincarnation: The Universal Return" was first published in *Chrysalis*, journal of the Swedenborg Foundation, New York City, Autumn 1987.

"The Soul, Hidden and Manifest" was first published in an edited form under the title "Now You See It, Now You Don't: The Soul" in *Chrysalis*, Winter 1985.

"Uses: A Way of Personal and Spiritual Growth" was first published as a chapter in *The Presence of Other Worlds*, by Wilson Van Dusen, Harper and Row, 1974.

"Self-Reflection in the Forging of a Person" was first published as a chapter in *Experiences in Being*, Bernice Marshall, Editor, Brooks/Cole Publishing Co., Belmont, Calif., 1971.

"Exploring Swedenborg's Dream Journal" was first published as the introduction to *Journal of Dreams*, by Emanuel Swedenborg, Swedenborg Foundation, 1986.

"Meditation" was first published in the journal *New Philosophy*, Vol. 78, No. 4, Swedenborg Scientific Association, Bryn Athyn, Penn., 1975.

"The Psalm of What Is" was first published in *Psychedelic Review*, No. 6, 1965.

J. Appleseed & Co.
3200 Washington St.
San Francisco, CA 94115

Contents

Foreword

Wilson Van Dusen occupies a unique and effective position among the large field of writers who have explored that tantalizing mountain of spirituality wrought and bequeathed by Emanuel Swedenborg. Dr. Van Dusen's own diverse areas of experience and expertise—science and religion, poetry and psychology—provide him a wide lens for taking in the full terrain, or at least a goodly portion of it. As a self-described mystic, he has made his reputation by approaching Swedenborg's writings boldly and with fearless reliance upon self-reference. The result has been a "voice" in Swedenborgiana emphasizing personal spiritual experience that has gained an enthusiastic following which appears to be even stronger outside the several walls of the organized Swedenborgian groups than within them.

The call keeps coming in for more books to supplement his two highly acclaimed works from the decade of the Seventies. To meet this demand and to seek new audiences for Dr. Van Dusen's often provocative, always challenging interpretive work with both Swedenborg and spiritual practice, I have worked in consultation with the author in culling these selections from his corpus of some four-score articles, essays, and chapters in numerous publications going back to the mid-Fifties. More than he knows, I am grateful to the Rev. Dr. William R. Woofenden, whose ever-watchful eye enabled this book to be much improved in numerous places.

James F. Lawrence
Editor

A Mystic Looks at Swedenborg

> THE DOCTRINES SIMPLY ARE NOT MUCH USE TO ME UNLESS I KNOW WHAT IT IS IN MY OWN EXPERIENCE THAT THEY ARE TALKING ABOUT.
>
> — George Dole, from *Messenger* review of *Arcana Coelestia*

> . . . THERE IS THE CLOSEST RELATION BETWEEN THE MODE OF APPREHENSION AND THE THING APPREHENDED.
>
> — Gabriel Marcel, from *Creative Fidelity*

I use the word *mystic* in its simplest and most basic sense. A mystic is one who experiences God. There are other associated meanings and very complex analyses in religious encyclopedias, but they all rest in this—the experience of God. Some might ask, "Don't all people experience God?" And I would answer yes, but many are not aware of it. The mystic is aware of it.

Perhaps I need to underline the verb *experience*. It is quite a bit more than simply thinking about God or addressing God. God becomes manifest, obvious. And by using the present tense I also mean to imply that the experience tends to be ongoing. Having experienced God once, one acquires a taste for it. The mystic learns how to find his or her way back into that communion.

In this essay I'll cite my own experience merely because it is handy for me, with some reference to the experience of others. My aim is to make the spiritual experience familiar enough to be recognizable to the reader. After establishing this base we will then see how this is reflected in Swedenborg. The parallel is not simply in the fact that Swedenborg talks about God. Most theological writing concerns God, but most also seems quite flat and unmystical to me. On the other hand, certain music, literature, paintings, and other art forms easily bring me back to the experience of the Divine. The relevance of mystical experience to Swedenborg's own has more to do with a mode of experiencing than with more content matter.

The Nature of Mysticism

If someone asked when I first became aware that I was a mystic, I would date it to early adolescence. We lived on the top floor of several flats, and I soon discovered I could climb a ladder to the roof. In the crowded world of San Francisco I found that the rooftop offered me an expansive private world. The dusk of evening was always the nicest time. Lights were dimming and my thoughts soared. I came back repeatedly to the feeling of the oneness of things. All the city lights, all the dusky shapes, all the sounds were One Life. I knew also I was this One Life looking at and admiring the One Life. The basic feeling was awe or reverence. No matter what the difficulties of the day, in the evening, under the stars, it was indeed wonder-full.

On the front of the roof was a curved decoration. It was high enough so that I could lean on it and safely look down on the street. I remember lovingly touching the tar paper with awe. The very reality of substance seemed miraculous. I heard the sound of a distant dog bark. I was in such a sense of oneness that it was as though I heard my own life. I remember hearing a screen door squeak and slam shut somewhere, and with that simple sound I knew the design of creation. I remember swearing to myself that no matter what happens in life, I would always come back to the peace of evening. And, in a real sense, by writing of it I am back to that peace. I was so awestruck by the wonder of existence. There was also no sense of ego—no me versus it. Me and it were one.

Reverence is the term that would come to me now to describe the experience, but it would not have then. I had yet to learn that religion and God really existed. My father was an atheist and my mother disdained all religion, even though she was raised a Catholic. She had had a hard life. She had said many times, "If there was a God, he would be unspeakably horrible." I had heard church services on the radio, but they didn't impress me. The preachers sounded like pompous salesmen, selling the Word instead of cars.

At that time my experience was nameless. I can remember the book that first suggested to me I was not alone, that there were others out there with similar experiences. My first five-cent book purchase was Thomas Troward's *Edinburgh Lectures in Mental Science*.[1] I was struck by the wonder of money, if it could buy treasures like that. Thomas Troward was a member of the New Thought Movement. For the first time I saw echoes of my experience in print: "But because the universal personalness is the root of all individual personalities, it finds its highest expression in response to those who realize its personal nature."[2] Yes, that's it. A spiritual moment is immensely personal. I didn't hear any of the religious radio programs say that. "He must realize that the whole process is that of bringing the universal within the grasp of the individual by raising the individual to the level of the universal, and not vice-versa."[3] Yes, yes! So when I see the design of all in the sound of a screen door, it is the universal. Everything I saw, heard, or touched spoke of the universal. It was a great comfort to discover, at last, that I was not alone. Others have realized the same thing.

But, in a way, the experience was frustrating. It was like standing on the edge of a vast sea of mystery, feeling that it was all here, yet I wanted

1. Thomas Troward, *Edinburgh Lectures in Mental Science* (New York: Dodd, Mead, 1909).

2. Ibid., p. 50.

3. Ibid., p. 54.

something specific. I'd ask the universal for guidance in my life, and then chide it for its lack of specificity. All wasn't enough; I wanted something more!

But the idea of the oneness of all things took firm root. It found countless echoes later, in the ecologist's concern for life, in the universality of humanity, for examples. When I was young one of my favorite fantasies was that I was making speeches to the world on peace and the fellowship of humanity. I had a whole binder of what seemed, at the time, like very inspired lectures. In later years I burned them as a bit too adolescent to keep. But it still happens that the theme of the universality of life can easily bring tears to my eyes. It is something I feel so strongly that my reason has to stand aside. I know I'm me and you're you, and that much separates and distinguishes us. But that's the job of reason, to cut things up and set them apart. It doesn't matter. I've experienced the oneness of All. It became apparent to me that life could either be taken apart or experienced as a one. The experience of oneness was the more fundamental, satisfying, and powerful. It was the truth. All this taking apart is secondary, flat, and trivial in comparison.

You might wonder what the mystical experience does to personal identity. Sensing the All, would I not be greater than most who don't do this? Not in the least. Sensing the All, I am the equal of all—the equal of tar paper, a dog's bark, and stars. I would say the experience relaxes the personal identity down to the point where it doesn't matter. Later I was impressed by the Greek expression *En to Pan,* "the One is the All."

Over the years it gradually dawned on me that my experience was religious and that the Universal One was another name for God. You see, I had these kinds of experiences before names, even before speech or words. Though I began this essay with an account from adolescence, I can recall an experience all the way back in infancy, when I was still in a crib, possibly around the age of one. I lay there with my head turned to the side. Sunlight was streaming though the window. Motes of dust floated and turned in the beam of sunlight. Fixing on them I saw endless rainbows of color. The feeling was of ecstasy and awe. Later I learned in my study of psychoanalysis that this identification with everything is common in children—that it was a childish quality I'd apparently failed to outgrow! Be that as it may, I found the roots of mystical experience can exist before words, concepts, religious training, before all the obscuring machinations of the world. I suspect these experiential roots are pretty much universal; they occur in all people. But in various ways our education and acculturation can obscure them. The center can be forgotten.

In some way my memory was turned around. My experience of the All became my foundation. Later, people were surprised when I said I could far more easily doubt my own existence than I could doubt God's. My own existence seems variable, hard to grasp, doubtful, and really trivial. The All is everything. Perhaps by some bit of luck (another term is *God's grace*) I retained the memory of what others also knew and misplaced or forgot. In some way I feel obliged to described the mystical experience so that others may recover it.

So here I will describe my adult way of returning to it, which may also work for you. I've been in and out of mystical experiences so often that it has finally become clear how to find my way back. It can be done anywhere, at any time. But there are certain necessities. I cannot be rushed nor in pain. The mood is one of no hurry, endless time. I feel very open. I'll accept whatever is given. It is the opposite of making demands on God. The mood is one of openness and play. Just for the fun I feel like stopping here and admiring the flowers. Long ago I discovered it is the heart of aesthetic experience. How best to appreciate what is before you but by stopping, looking, being open to what is suggested?

I had a group of alcoholic women contend that this could not be done within the bare walls of an institution. So I had them dwell intensely on the floor. One noticed a crack in the cement, and in describing what it suggested to her, she came to a tearful description of her life pattern. Everything reveals if we are patient with it.

The whole of existence is like looking at a painting. I am regarding Van Gogh's second self-portrait. At first I take in the obvious details: his face is angular and bearded; his clothes are rude, those of a peasant; the blue background swirls around his head with areas of chaos. There's a remarkable, quiet intensity in the face. Though closed-mouthed and mute, the intensity is almost wild, brooding. And this is the center of the man. He has painted his very nature. I empathize with the power of his struggle. In the mystical mood I allow all there is to speak, to affect me. If I had to train mystics I would certainly consider using art appreciation as a first step. For in it is the foundation of letting things reveal themselves to you.

But you may say this is merely aesthetic and not religious. The aesthetic is a step into the doorway of the religious. Its basic attitude is one of appreciation. It leads to awe and respect. It is the practice of openness to what is here. Like the aesthetic person, the mystic is in an appreciation of things as they are. This moment is perfect. It is all here, all there is.

There is a tremendous nowness to the mystical experience. It is as though all there ever was passes through this present into all there ever will be. One rests in such a moment. Questions have no place. Doubts are absent. Here, thus, it *is*. I once asked God for a sign of his existence. God answers in direct knowing, beyond words. His answer was in effect, "Is not the whole of existence sign enough?" Well, yes, that's a pretty good one: existence—yes, I'd call that a substantial sign!

My existence is among these signs. So sometimes I just look at and admire my hand. Interesting form. Skin a little wrinkled because I'm aging. A real marvel how it is animated. Look at it writing here. Marvelous. I wonder what words are and how my hand works. I am mystery, looking at mystery, appreciating mystery. The very essence of mystical experience is to appreciate this fully—what is. Does it plague me that I am a mystery? No. I appreciate it. How far this is from egotism or Swedenborg's term *proprium*. No egotism, because I know beyond my understanding that the same life animates the pine tree in my backyard that animates me. What a delightfully pervasive mystery. What an honor to be an equal to pine trees, grass, and clouds.

I've described the mood and attitude that leads to mystical experience—taking the time to be open and thoroughly appreciate what is before you. But there are also deeper hallmarks of the mystical experience. Meaning is given, noetic. You suddenly realize something that is prior to thought, before any reasoning. You might just *know* that

God is present. If someone asks how or where, you would have nothing to point to. This knowing can vary from a gentle suggestion to an absolute certainty. Outside that experience the subject himself can doubt it. "Was God really present?" But during the noetic givenness of knowing, doubt or questioning is not possible. I've even formulated my biggest questions and written them down, only to find my own sheet of questions rather ridiculous during the experience of God. One of the reasons I've written for many years and barely said anything of this experience is that it is sacred and beyond doubt.

I recall a woman who had a sudden, unexpected experience of God lasting probably less than five seconds. She described it to a nun, who remarked, "You probably just had a digestive upset." The woman spent decades studying mysticism and trying to return to the experience, but after the nun's rejection she rarely told anyone of it. She now trains priests in the deeper aspects of religious experience. The mystical experience is so characterized by direct knowing that I'd call into question an experience where God talks aloud to a person.

The experience is up through the core of one's being. Words are not necessary. I once saw an angelic figure with wings crossed in front as though to conceal something. I wondered what was concealed. Suddenly the answer came flooding in, but not in words. I was just given to know. The hidden secret was that there is no death. Nowhere in the whole of existence is there death. You are struck with not only the words but also the full ramifications of them. People think of death as real. The angel revealed the deeper truth; no one ever dies. And like waves and ripples the full ramifications play on the consciousness. In Raymond Moody's cases of people who "died" on the operating table and later were revived, many reported meeting a radiant figure who communicated by direct mind-to-mind knowing.[4] A parallel in ordinary experience is the way lovers sense so much before anything is said. In sharp contrast, when people who are hallucinating meet demons of hell, they *talk* endlessly but they say little! The more powerful the feeling that goes with direct knowing, the more I'd suspect it is just plain truth. Often in these experiences symbols are given, and at the

4. Raymond Moody, *Life After Life* (Atlanta, GA.: Mockingbird Books, 1975).

same time the meanings of the symbols are given. A meaning can be so nonverbal that the person receiving it may have difficulty putting it into words. In these cases I'd say it is therapeutic and useful to draw what was seen and attempt to extract and put into words all the information. Otherwise the ordinary consciousness may later look at what was given and translate it into something much less significant than it was at the time (e.g., "I saw an angel and I guess it meant so and so"). But going back to the experience, one finds it packed with meaning. I was once given a simple hand gesture of two fingers extended and its meaning. I was thrilled years later to see it in an old painting in the Eastern Orthodox Church.

William James writes about the noetic:

> ALTHOUGH SO SIMILAR TO STATES OF FEELING, MYSTICAL STATES SEEM TO THOSE WHO EXPERIENCE THEM TO ALSO BE STATES OF KNOWLEDGE. THEY ARE STATES OF INSIGHT INTO DEPTHS OF KNOWLEDGE. THEY ARE STATES OF INSIGHT INTO DEPTHS OF TRUTH UNPLUMBED BY THE DISCURSIVE INTELLECT. THEY ARE ILLUMINATIONS, REVELATIONS, FULL OF SIGNIFICANCE AND IMPORTANCE, ALL INARTICULATE THOUGH THEY REMAIN; AND AS A RULE THEY CARRY WITH THEM A CURIOUS SENSE OF AUTHORITY FOR AFTERTIME.[5]

William James also describes the mystical experience as "ineffable," or impossible to describe in words. I would not go so far as to say this. With care one can describe the state. It's just that one can't fully convey the state in words because, as he says, it is more like states of feeling than of intellect.

The Several Paths Are One Path

Having experienced a remarkable state, I was naturally curious to look at what the world's literature had to say of it. There are a number of

5. William James, *The Varieties of Religious Experience* (New York: Modern Library, 1902), p. 371.

scholarly compilations—collections and commentaries on what mystics have to say. Other than a few touching quotes from real mystics, these commentaries fall quite flat for me. Those writing them often draw conclusions that are just untrue, possibly because they haven't had the experience. They also tend to make a basically simple and direct experience quite complex, constructing stages, and stages within stages of the experience. Yet the real experience is terribly simple and straightforward.

In great contrast, the work of actual mystics often soars for me. Among these I'd list Plotinus, Khalil Gibran, Saint Theresa of Lisieux, Jakob Böhme, the Zen Buddhists, some Hindu works, and Omar Khayyám. Notice that this listing ranges across several religions. Mystics are dealing with universal truth revealed in most, and perhaps all, religions. Even though the content of these authors seems different—Gibran is in verse; Saint Theresa describes her relationship to Christ; Plotinus the Greek, like Jakob Böhme, presents a soaring intellectual understanding—they have the power of one who has been there.

In my experience mystics have no difficulty recognizing other mystics. Because their eye is on the universal they see beyond historical and doctrinal differences. I've often been asked by individuals whether their experience of God was true. Let me cite an unusual case to illustrate the process. I was at a Christian church gathering at a camp in the mountains. A minister's wife indicated she wanted to speak to me. As a practiced clinical psychologist I could see that great feeling was involved. She hesitated to speak. Finally I got her to tell her story.

One day a friend came to see her, bearing the message that her deceased father loved her. Suddenly the situation opened up for her. She knew beyond doubt that this man, in the body of a known friend, was actually God, and God came to repair the relationship with her father. She had been emotionally alienated from her father. She asked me if this was a true experience of God, even though inwardly she knew beyond doubt it was. I felt a tremendous impact in her story. We both struggled unsuccessfully with tears. My response was that her story had the ring of truth to it, though I had never before seen the form of her experience—God coming in the body of a friend. God is able to come in any form, even the form of a friend. The incident essentially did good: it brought her into loving relationship with her father.

The woman's story had all of the hallmarks I look for in a genuine experience of God. People hesitate to speak. What they have to say is powerfully sacred to them. It is the opposite of bragging: they would rather say nothing happened than to have the sacred rejected. The experience is linked to powerful feeling, which indicates to me that it comes from beyond mere intellect, from beyond the manipulations of consciousness. It is as though the very source of life is touched and shaken. Finally I ask whether the experience does good. If so, I believe it is from God. I affirmed, as she already inwardly felt, that the experience was quite genuine.

What you often find, as was true of her, is that the mystical experience can be so powerful and otherworldly that the subject is somewhat at a loss as to what to do with it. I saw she was having difficulty integrating the experience. She said she went to the bishop of her church afterward and he so discredited the experience that she swore to herself never to speak again of religious feeling in church! I took the opposite tack. Given that God was trying to repair the bond between her and her father, I asked that she prayerfully dwell on the love between them. I reinforce the trend in the experience. I try to act in concert with the tendencies shown by God. Countless bishops and psychotherapists could not kill the inner life of her experience. But in a few moments I could strike a sentient chord merely by recognizing and reinforcing the quality of the experience given her.

I relate this incident to illustrate several things. I believe mystics can easily see and empathize with genuine experience in others regardless of religious differences, no matter how unusual the form. I also think it something of a crime for someone to invalidate the depth of experience in others. It would have been far better if the bishop had said, "I don't know if your experience was really of God," for actually he didn't know.

Would I call this woman a mystic? Potentially, yes. She had had only one experience, but treating this one in a positive way would encourage her to open to others. She was just at the entrance of the house; she had yet to move in and become comfortable in the house. This woman's story also illustrates that the mystical experience is not totally ineffable, beyond description. Difficult to convey, yes; impossible, no. Moreover, in attempting to do so, others who hear of it might rethink their own sacred experiences and renew their belief in the wonders that have been given to them.

Follow if you will, a fantasy of mine. Suppose I am able to encourage many people to describe their sacred experiences. I compile and publish a newsletter of these and we convene to discuss them. In these meetings the mood is one of acceptance of and respect for even the tiniest traces of sacredness in each other's experience. Because one describes, others recognize similar experiences in themselves. Because we accept and express and share these, new experiences arise and are shared. Mystical experience becomes common and we are able to explore the length and breadth of it. A fantasy? Not entirely.

I've seen Teen Challenge sessions in which a similar situation occurred. All of the members present had been drug addicts picked up while down and out on the street. Because the group had expectations that the experience of Christ would occur, it did frequently. I recall one addict saying he watched in amazement as his hands poured heroin down the toilet. In that moment he knew that Christ controlled him.

I have also seen Teen Challenge members speak to religious groups and frighten them. Most people's experience of religion is cool, rational, controlled. These people really believe, and they frighten people of a cool religion. For a similar reason in the history of mysticism it was fairly common for mystics to write anonymously (as did Swedenborg at first) or to come into conflict with the church (Teilhard de Chardin), or to write their experiences in a partly disguised form ("The Rubáiyát" of Omar Khayyám).

So let me alter my fantasy above. Only mystics (of any religion) may enter our circle, and we share with each other only. But the underlying theme of my fantasy is that we share and respect experiences of God and thereby encourage others to recognize it in their life. In this day and age, I find that what is missing from and repressed in many people's lives is the sacred, not sexuality, as some maintain.

Why? At first, one might suggest we tend to hold back a sacred experience because we don't want others to scoff at it. The bishop's put-down of the woman discussed previously is a good example. The experience is particularly delicate if one has had only one or a few experiences. This is a partial reason for repressing the sacred. But there is another reason that has to do with the inward nature of the experience. What opens up in the person is the deepest root of life itself. It *is* one's life. Would we hand a scalpel to a passing stranger to perform surgery on us? The experience is our life, our very life. It often repels even the skeptical probing of the subjects themselves. That is, the experience can seem alien and incredible to even the person who has it. There is a great difference between the person who is moved in one sacred moment and the same person in the workaday world. In the light of day, that transcendent experience can be questioned and doubted by the subject who had it. Did it really happen? Was that God, or digestive upset? It is uncomfortable to doubt it. It is like pinching oneself unnecessarily. So an uneasy peace settles.

I believe that in the most inward sense there is a natural protection around the sacred. At the very worst the experience will totally disappear from memory rather than leave the sacred to be permanently questioned. So the barriers to assault on it are both internal and external. I don't want it to be laughed at so I won't tell others. It is somehow wrong even for me to question it, so I'll not do so. It takes respect for the sacred by one person to open it up to expression in another. The woman who reacted to the bishop's put-down wasn't simply a petulant woman. The sacred protects itself, so she resolved never to expose real religious feeling in church again. I don't fully understand how the sacred protects itself. But I suspect if we could see its full ramifications we'd be surprised at its artful, in-depth protection. I am so convinced that the sacred is the very root and source of life itself that I'm sure some have died rather than expose it (e.g., the early Christian martyrs). The doubts of others are rather easy to fend off: simply keep quiet about it. Internal doubt is another matter.

I would not be at all surprised to learn that one day madness itself comes from turning against the early budding of mystical experience in a person. Why do I say this? Because in madness I often see a strange tangle of essentially religious elements turned back on itself. It would be better not to have the experience of God than to harm it in any way. At the very least the person who has it would be better off to leave the possibility of its reality open and seek out its possible good than to turn away.

There are several other hallmarks of the mystical experience. One is a strong sense of the familiar, no matter how unusual the outer situation. Once I was watching a play. An actor said, "I've returned as I promised." Suddenly the play opened up. I felt that God spoke through the actor, and I was in tears that God had returned. I've walked in ruined churches that I'd not seen before and suddenly had an overwhelming feeling of the familiar. In the ruins of a monks' abbey I was suddenly familiar with the monks and their devoted labor of building the church. Sometimes when interviewing a person it also occurs that suddenly, again, there is the familiar God in them. The feeling is very pleasant, like coming home after a long trip. It often comes to me when I'm with people talking about sharing with others or about universal humanity. The full mystical experience leaves a very broad signature on the inner life that then finds itself expressed in many ways. The sense of familiarity is so consistent that I would question whether the experience of *déjà vu* might not be a part of mysticism. I would encourage those with *déjà vu* to reflect deeply on what they recognize in the experience. Try to bring up and examine all the feelings. It may be a tiny precursor to the mystical. I was once talking to a neurotic woman. There was something in her very preened formality. Suddenly I felt the essence of Egyptian religion. It is difficult to describe, but it has to do with reaching and preserving the contact with the Eternal. The changeless is close to the sacred—so it was necessary to preserve the body. A religion that seemed foreign to me was suddenly familiar. It revered the changeless, which is an approach to the Eternal.

There is another aspect of the mystical experience that seems to be consistently misunderstood. It is as though we must die to ourselves in order to see God. This leads to all sorts of efforts to overcome the self. This is an impossible paradox, for the one struggling against the self turns out to be simply the self. In a way, the self is actually intensified by the effort to get rid of it. The truth is that in a mystical experience there is an expansion of the self—quite the opposite. It is as though God is always present and is the root and source of our very life. God need only expand our awareness to come into consciousness. The relaxed openness is part of allowing this to happen, allowing the source to speak. The love of God calls forth the experience.

There is another related problem. I've wondered if I should tell you of my great visions. Readers might compare their little visions to my great ones and conclude that they have not yet reached the same level. This is a kind of spiritual nonsense. Like Swedenborg,[6] we become disappointed if our vision doesn't knock us clear out of bed. It is the doubting little self that demands miracles, lightning to strike this very instant. What is wrong is that this competitive race for the biggest vision overlooks all the tiny ones. It is loving appreciation of the tiny ones that may (God willing) prepare us for a bigger vision. A key to understanding here is that we really can't (repeat, *can't*) make God come give us a giant experience. This is a presumption against the very nature of the spiritual. Learn to appreciate the absolute wonder that you already have. We breathe, don't we? Isn't it a marvelous process that we take in and expel the world regularly, whether we think of it or not? I wonder if there is meaning beyond oxygenating the blood. The Hindus have described a way to God that includes principally focusing on breathing. Earlier I described a mystical experience in simply looking at and wondering at the life that cleverly moves my hands, I know not how. Looking at and enjoying the wonder of nature is a universal experience of humankind. Beware of asking God for big visions, just to prove he exists. Having had one vision, you may tend to doubt it and ask for one more bigger one, and so on. Finally you will die, and it is hoped that the vision you have then will at last be big enough!

---

6. Wilson Van Dusen, *Swedenborg's Journal of Dreams* (New York: Swedenborg Foundation, 1986).

Both the effort to overcome the self and the demand for big visions are common spiritual traps. God comes by expanding your present awareness. Learn to see the miracles here all the time. The very essence of the mystical experience is to appreciate what is here now. That is becoming a child again—finding amazingly beautiful something as small as a dried-up leaf that fell from a tree.

Some may conclude that the mystical can be sensed in the beautiful things in life (i.e., nature) but not in the ugly things. Not so. I have reflected on rubbish and garbage heaps and found wonders in them. Some put a big boundary between the things made by God (i.e., nature) and those made by human beings. In this dichotomy human creations are low and nature's high. This seems foolish to me. I am so aware that God designed the people who make things, that I am most anxious to watch science's discoveries and the unfolding of clever electronic gadgets. If you look for God, he may be found anywhere.

It would be fair to ask what the mystic ultimately discovers. Swedenborg's writings contain some of the better descriptions.

Swedenborg's Mysticism

> I CANNOT BUT OPEN UP THOSE THINGS OF THE WORD THAT ARE CALLED MYSTICAL, THAT IS, ITS INTERIOR THINGS. . . .
>
> — Emanuel Swedenborg (*Arcana Coelestia* 4923)

It came as a considerable surprise to me to learn that there is a tradition among students of Swedenborg's religious writings that Swedenborg is not a mystic. It is only too apparent to a mystic that his works are a major contribution to this literature, and mystics have freely referred to him as one of their own. Swedenborg's spiritual writings define mysticism in a way that inescapably makes Swedenborg a mystic. How is it, then, that some of his followers say, with earnest conviction, that he is not a mystic? We will look at what mysticism precisely is and how this error arose. We will also see how his religious works define mysticism and how this compares with the current accepted meaning. This is not a mere quibble over a term. At its least it implies a misunderstanding of mysticism. At its worst it may involve a misunderstanding of the very nature of Swedenborg's writings themselves.

The definition of mysticism has two conflicting currents. One, which we will call the scholarly definition, reflects the actual experience of mystics. The other, which we will call the layperson's definition, stands outside the experience and basically says it doesn't make sense. This confusion of opposing definitions is quite old and extends back before Swedenborg's time. Many dictionaries will reflect both views. The core of the scholarly definitions is the experience of union with the Divine. The core of the layperson's definitions is whatever is occult, mysterious, unclear, or involved with spirits.

Followers who use the layperson's definition are more than happy to say Swedenborg wasn't interested in the occult, which is true, and hence not a mystic. The very rationality and clarity of his spiritual writings would seem to militate against their being mystical. Let us look at the dictionary definitions. The closer the dictionary is to the popular mind, the more likely it will reflect the unprofessional layperson's definition as well as the scholarly. Scholarly religious dictionaries tend to drop the popular misconception altogether and deal only with the real internal meaning of the experience. The following reflects more of the popular misconception:

> Mystical, 1. mystic; occult. 2. of or pertaining to mystics or mysticism: mystical writings. 3. spiritually symbolic. 4. rare: obscure in meaning; mysterious.[7]

Swedenborg's own definition was the third one above—"spiritually symbolic." This same dictionary, reflecting the popular conception, says of the word *mystic:* "known only to the initiated; of occult power or significance; of obscure or mysterious character. . . ." It is from this aspect that followers of Swedenborg's religious writings wanted to dissociate themselves, for these works are eminently rational and clear. Another dictionary almost overlooks this popular misconception:

---

7. *Random House Dictionary of the English Language* (New York: Random House, 1966).

> Mystical 1: having a spiritual meaning or reality, or the like, neither apparent to the senses nor obvious to the intelligence; symbolical; as, the church is the mystical body of Christ. 2: of, resulting from, or manifesting an individual's direct communion with God, through contemplation, vision, an inner light, or the like; as, mystical rapture. 3: now rare: unintelligible; cryptic.[8]

Notice that the definitions, "obscure in meaning, mysterious" and "cryptic" are now seen as rare.

It is through communion with the Divine that direct spiritual understanding is given, which is often symbolic and difficult to translate into ordinary terms for others. The difficulty of conveying the internal experience to others has made it seem obscure to outsiders. Then, to add to the confusion, there have been the pseudomystics who use the term for self-aggrandizement, as though to say, "This is mystical and too deep for your understanding, but of course I understand it!"

The very authoritative *Hastings Enclyclopedia of Religion and Ethics* goes to the heart of the matter:

> MYSTICISM—"Mysticism," in common speech-usage, is a word of very uncertain connotation. It has in recent times been used as an equivalent for two characteristically different German words: *Mystizismus*, which stands for the cult of the supernatural, for theosophical pursuits, for a spiritualistic exploitation of physical research; and *Mystik*, which stands for immediate experience of a divine-human intercourse and relationship. The word "mysticism" has, furthermore, been commonly used to cover both (1) the first-hand experience of direct intercourse with God and (2) the theologico-metaphysical doctrine of the soul's possible union with Absolute Reality, i.e., with God. It would be conducive to clarity to restrict the word "mysticism" to the latter signifi-

8. *Webster's Collegiate Dictionary* (Springfield, Mass.: Merriman, 1942).

> cance, namely, as an equivalent for the German word *Mystik*, and as designating the historic doctrine of the relationship and potential union of the human soul with Ultimate Reality, and to use the term "mystical experience" for direct intercourse with God.
>
> First-hand, or mystical, experience is primarily a psychological question; the doctrine of mysticism is essentially a metaphysical problem. Mystical experience is as old as humanity, is not confined to any one racial stock, is undoubtedly one of the original grounds of personal religion, and does not stand or fall with the truth or falsity of the metaphysically formulated doctrine of mysticism. Mystical experience is marked by the emergence of a type of consciousness.[9]

The more than twenty pages of tiny print make no further reference to the layperson's definition. In spite of what the author, Rufus Jones, a noted scholar of mysticism, would like to see, the term *mysticism* is used most often for the experience. The literature on the qualities of the experience is vast; that on the doctrinal aspects is relatively scant. In fact Swedenborg's spiritual writings are an unusual combination of the experiential and the doctrinal aspects of mysticism. In brief, then, the most accepted definition of mysticism refers to all aspects of the experience of conjunction or union with the Divine and secondarily to doctrines about this. This is the sense in which I use the term.

It is relatively easy to demonstrate that all those who have said Swedenborg was not a mystic used the now-rare and not really acceptable layperson's definition. None of them were trying to say that his writings do not deal with the experience of the Divine—the core of the accepted meaning of mysticism. My sources are not complete, but a couple of references will illustrate the point.

Herbert C. Small in 1929 did one of the more impressive antimystical articles. A few quotes will show he is using the layperson's definition: "Mysticism is the main cause of all religious superstition

9. *Hastings Encyclopedia of Religion and Ethics* (New York: Scribners, 1961).

and phantasy. . . . These experiences run the entire gamut of magic, spiritism, occultism, Holy Ghostism, theosophy . . . and what not. . . . [Swedenborg] sought no occult source, and employed none."[10] Small's complete argument can't be put down so easily. Basically he says that mystics are led by their own intuition, which becomes an authority higher than the Word. This is simply not true. There are countless mystics who revere the Word because they have experienced something of its inner sense. But his is the view of the one outside the experience. Indeed, he feels those who have the experience are incompetent to judge it; only one outside it can be a proper judge! "It is quite useless in most cases to rely on definitions of mysticism as given by its devotees, for they have no knowledge of its true nature."[11] Standing outside the experience, he links it to all excesses of self leading and falling into occult and mysterious falsities. If, for his use of the term, one substitutes the now-accepted meaning of the term—the experience of the Divine—then all his arguments would fail; for he could not say the one who has *no* experience of the Divine is better able to judge the worth of the experience than one who *has known* God. There would be no linking to "spiritism," for the experience of God is not the experience of spirits. He emphasized Swedenborg the scientist, collecting and analyzing facts, but he had to admit Swedenborg was led of the Lord, which is precisely what the now-accepted definition of mysticism means.

In a recent example Brian Kingslake also disclaims Swedenborg as a mystic.[12] Though he finds many similarities between Swedenborg's life and that of other prominent mystics, he sees a difference in that Swedenborg's religious works are rational. Mysticism is nonrational; this is again from the layperson's definition. As a matter of fact, mystical writings vary across the whole spectrum of clarity and rationality. Basically, mysticism, or the experience of God, is irrational to those outside the experience. It is rational, true, and clear to those in

10. Herbert Small, "What Is a Mystic?" *The Messenger* (1929), p. 340.

11. Ibid.

12. Brian Kingslake, "Was Swedenborg a Mystic?" *New Church Magazine* (1977); pp. 52ff.

the experience. It informs reason of higher truths. If Swedenborg had not clarified his experience beyond the *Spiritual Diary* he would appear to have been very irrational. The experience of God makes a higher sense. Seen in the whole of the world's mystical literature, Swedenborg's spiritual writings are perhaps near average for clarity or rationality. When you go to the heart of the meaning of mysticism—the experience of God—and substitute this for the word *mysticism*, then most of the arguments that Swedenborg was no mystic fall. He obviously had much experience of God and tried to teach us of this, which is precisely what being a mystic means. Some will find it clear and rational and others will not. The closer one is to a similar experience of the Divine, the clearer and more rational these works of Swedenborg will seem. For example, by comparison, Christ's teachings are perhaps even clearer and much of Böhme's works less clear.

The only perceptive use of mysticism I was able to find in the collateral literature was in Block's conclusion to her historical survey. Two quotes might entice some readers to review the whole chapter:

> The New Church in general has ignored the mystical side of religion, though it is absolutely inherent in the doctrine of influx—the entrance of God into the individual soul, as well as in the doctrine of perception, or interior reception of spiritual truth.[13]

> Perhaps after all the issue in the New Church is not the simple and obvious one between "fundamentalism" and "modernism," but the more ancient one between literalism and mysticism which has appeared in almost all the world's religions at various times.[14]

I suspect Block has her finger on the difficulty. I fear that there are natural and fundamentally different approaches to reality and human

13. Marguerite Block, *The New Church in the New World* (New York: Octagon, 1968), p. 393.

14. Ibid., p. 400.

experience reflected in her literalism versus mysticism, that even if Swedenborg were a classic mystic the literalists would not be able to discover this. But this is another whole large issue, whether any amount of doctrine can ever get us to break out of the shell of our inherent approach to reality.

The following will clarify the contrasting definitions of mysticism:

MYSTICISM

The outsider's position, layperson's rare meaning	*The inside experience, scholarly accepted definition*
Being led by every emotional whim	Being led by God
Concerned with spirits and other powers	Concerned with God alone
Irrational and mysterious	Rational, a higher understanding
Seen as contrary to the authority of Swedenborg's religious writings	Seen as reinforcing the authority of Swedenborg's religious writings
Each is a law unto himself	God rules all

What do Swedenborg's religious writings themselves say of mysticism? It is disturbing to me to think of all those who claim to stand on the authority of his writings and choose to overlook what they say of mysticism. Swedenborg uses the term *mystical* (*mysticus*) rarely, only fourteen times that I count in his work. In the Latin it means what is hidden or secret. He uses it in several related senses, which include both the layperson's and the scholarly uses.

Sometimes he uses it to disparage the pretentiously obscure (*Arcana Coelestia* 5223, 7296),* or the irrational, such as the mystic dogma of

* It was Swedenborg's practice to number his paragraphs for easy reference.

the trinity (*True Christian Religion* 169) or when he refers to the mystical and enigmatical faith of present-day theology (*True Christian Religion* 351).

At other times he uses it to mean the sacred that is not understood and appreciated and hence rejected. Speaking of the science of representations and correspondences, which is often rejected, he writes:

> . . . HARDLY ANYONE IS WILLING TO BELIEVE THAT IT EXISTS, AND THEY WHO DO BELIEVE THIS, MERELY CALLED IT SOMETHING MYSTICAL THAT IS OF NO USE. — *Arcana Coelestia* 2763

> AND IF WHAT IS INTERNAL OR SPIRITUAL IS MERELY MENTIONED, THEY EITHER RIDICULE IT OR CALL IT MYSTICAL, CONSEQUENTLY, ALL CONJUNCTION BETWEEN THEM IS BROKEN, AND WHEN THIS IS BROKEN THE SPIRITUAL MAN SUFFERS GRIEVOUSLY AMONG THE MERELY NATURAL. — *Arcana Coelestia* 5022

> BUT WHAT IS MEANT THEREBY, CHRISTIANITY [NOW-A-DAYS] DOES NOT ENQUIRE BECAUSE IT PLACES THE CELESTIAL AND SPIRITUAL THINGS OF THE WORD IN ITS LITERAL SENSE, AND CALLS ITS INTERIOR THINGS MYSTICAL FOR WHICH IT DOES NOT CARE.
>
> — *Arcana Coelestia* 9688

But these are his peripheral uses of the word *mystical*. In his strongest and most unambiguous uses he refers to the interior spiritual and celestial sense of the Word. Note the power of these statements:

> I CANNOT BUT OPEN UP TO THOSE THINGS OF THE WORD THAT ARE CALLED MYSTICAL, THAT IS, ITS INTERIOR THINGS, WHICH ARE THE SPIRITUAL AND CELESTIAL THINGS OF THE LORD'S KINGDOM.
>
> — *Arcana Coelestia* 4923

> THE MYSTICAL THINGS WHICH SOME SEEK IN THE WORD, ARE NOTHING ELSE THAN THE SPIRITUAL AND CELESTIAL SENSES.
>
> — *Sacred Scripture* 21

THE ARCANA OF WISDOM OF THE THREE HEAVENS CONTAINED IN [THE WORD] ARE THE MYSTICAL THINGS OF WHICH MANY HAVE SPOKEN. — *Apocalypse Explained* 1079

"I AM IN THE FATHER, AND THE FATHER IN ME." THIS IS THE MYSTICAL UNION OF WHICH MANY SPEAK.

— *Arcana Coelestia* 2004

Paragraph 4923 of *Arcana Coelestia* is worth reading in its entirety. Very clearly Swedenborg says the holy and the mystical that many felt existed in the Word, and for which they search, is nothing other than the interior of the Word, which he describes.

Does Swedenborg's definition of the mystical as the internal of the Word accord with the present-day scholarly definition? It is fully in accord if you are careful of what is meant. If one said "the experience of the internal sense," then there would be no doubt. The internal of the Word is the life of God. Experience of this internal sense is the experience of the Divine. I make this proviso so that one does not mistakenly think a mere knowledge of this internal sense brings one into the spiritual and celestial, which is the internal of the Word. Some kind of living involvement in the internal sense is necessary, an involvement that leads to uses and charity. To me, one of my more significant discoveries was the way Swedenborg personally invested himself in his study of the *Bible*.[15] This went beyond "knowledge of" to entering into the "life of" the internal. If one is thinking of a living participation in the internal sense of the Word, then Swedenborg's definition of the mystical accords with the modern scholarly meaning of mysticism. Can we then say that the person who "cannot but open up those things of the Word that are called mystical" is not a mystic?

There is a larger sense in which Swedenborg was clearly a mystic, a sense that breaks out of the limitations of a single word he actually didn't use very often. In the accepted positive scholarly sense, the

15. Wilson Van Dusen, "Another Key to Swedenborg's Development," *New Church Life* (1975), pp. 316–19.

mystic is simply one who has direct experience of the Divine. I doubt that any follower of Swedenborg's spiritual writings would say Swedenborg did not have direct experience of the Divine. Then he was a mystic. Mystics who write attempt to share their experience and its subsequent understandings with others. Contrary to the ideas of some that mysticism is irrational, most mystics who have written have produced quite rational works. In only a few places did Swedenborg say it was more than could be told or that it was not permitted yet to reveal. He made an eminent attempt to convey his direct experience and his consequent understandings. Have other mystics attempted to make as clear or rational a presentation? Indeed, yes. To those who want to pursue further the positive side of mysticism, I commend the works of Evelyn Underhill, especially her *Practical Mysticism.*[16] Her big volume *Mysticism*[17] leads one to the larger body of world literature on the subject.

Is there more mysticism in Swedenborg's religious writings than one man sharing his experience and findings of the Divine? I believe so, but this point cannot be proven in a limited space. If the mysticism of his writing lies preeminently in the internal sense of the Word, why is this sense presented to us? Is it to satisfy our curiosity, so we bystanders can look in at the dynamics of the life of God? I don't believe this is its purpose at all. Instead I submit that this was presented so we might come into the kingdom. If I had to describe Swedenborg's spiritual writings and their fundamental purpose in one line, it would be this: the writings are a clear presentation meant to be used by individuals to lead them into the life of God—as an actual part of their experience. His writings are rational, but that is their style, not preeminently their nature. Their nature and overwhelming purpose is to lead to God, which accounts for many aspects of their structure. So in this sense, not only are his writings the work of a mystic, they are meant to help create mystics, that is, to lead others to the Divine. I am quite in accord with the position of some regarding the sacredness and authority of Swedenborg's writings.

---

16. Evelyn Underhill, *Practical Mysticism* (New York: Dutton, 1915).

17. Evelyn Underhill, *Mysticism* (New York: Dutton, 1961).

Perhaps a few words on the general nature of mysticism in organized religion may help those to whom the connection of mysticism and Swedenborg's religious writings is new. Mystics, those who have contact with the Divine, have sprung up in all religions, all cultures, and all times. They express themselves variously in the forms and uses of their time, culture, and religion. Contrary to the outsider's idea that they may depart on any wild whim or intuition, persons with the expcrience of the Divine tend to be able to recognize this in others even across the barriers of time and circumstances. It is as though having touched the universal they can recognize others who have also done so. They tend to be socially useful, and in fact their uses may be the only outer expression of their experience of the Divine. Like Swedenborg, they tend to support *the old religious forms* but give them deeper meaning. It is not appropriate to rank them as to which is the greater mystic, for they are in no contest with each other. Rather we can say, "This one touches me and that one doesn't," which describes our own uniqueness. It is characteristic of mystics that they speak from experience rather than from speculation and past authority. It is often their lot to be seen as a threat to conventional religious authority, which may not dare claim an experience of God. Are mystics rare? Not really. Probably all persons have the experience of the Divine, often in childhood, but people differ in how conscious and ruling this experience is. Included in the scholarly definition is nature mysticism— the feeling of God present in nature—which must be a universal experience.

What is the evidence in Swedenborg's writings that he came into the experience of God? There is an even more critical interior question: What in his writings can lead you to God? To a mystic the signs of Swedenborg's contact with God are too legion to catalog, but I'll deal with the most general first. Throughout his writings Swedenborg is saying, "I have experienced. . . ." This is not said in an aggrandizing way. The whole *Spiritual Diary* contains his experiences. The "memorable relations" scattered through his late religious writings are experiences. He makes practically no reference to other scholars or theologians. On a few occasions he says the internal sense of the Bible was revealed by the Lord alone. No angels or spirits led him in this. Does he mean the Lord dictated the *Arcana Coelestia* word for word? I don't believe so. It was a noetic, direct-knowing experience. The experience has very pleasant inner verities, so one knows beyond doubt the real author. I am reminded of the phrase somewhere in the Bible that the sheep know their master. I picture a shepherd who lives all day with his sheep and sleeps with them at night. They know his very footsteps and smell. It is that kind of interior familiarity that exists in Swedenborg's writing.

Secondly, his writings not only come from experience but their real substance deals primarily with *human* experience. It is not as though the Divine and the human are two contents; there is but one content: the Divine/human. Swedenborg's is an immensely human view of theology. This may not be apparent to everyone. *Heaven and Hell* deals with angels, spirits, and demons. If they are human, don't they at least seem a bit removed from our world of humans? Not so. We have each experienced something of heaven and hell in this world. While we are in this life we each participate in societies of heaven and hell. That is, by our very nature, choices, or uses, we are intimately related to aspects of heaven and hell. Moreover I am struck how heaven and hell can also be understood as deeper aspects of mind. We not only exist by influx through the spiritual worlds, but also our interior design is in their form. For me, it has been a useful clarification to think how acts of mine and others may be heavenly or hellish.

The interior human aspect is throughout his writings. "Evidently it is these delights that rule the man's thoughts, and the thoughts are nothing apart from them; yet they seem to him to be nothing but thoughts; when in fact, thoughts are nothing but affections so composed into forms by his life's love as to be presented in light" (*Divine Providence* 199). It took a good deal of close observation to see that thoughts are formed of affections or feelings. An extensive part of the twelve-volume *Arcana Coelestia* has to do with the Lord's glorification, which is the model for the individual's spiritual development. But Swedenborg isn't merely dealing with the psychology of persons. His is a unique psychology thoroughly pervaded and informed by his spiritual experience. In two words it is a spiritual psychology. Because he is dealing with the very stuff of human existence, what he has to say is ultimately open to empirical test. I don't quite mean it is open to scientific test, because science can only deal with what is external. But I do mean it is open to test and confirmation by individuals. My essay on *Uses*[18] (see elsewhere in this book) is an example of bringing one of Swedenborg's core doctrines into personal experience, where the individual can see for oneself if it is true.

How is it that a boy's early experiences of wonder could eventually teach him to respect Swedenborg? For me the whole of religion is like a single tree. Religions are branches and the sects are leaves. We can concentrate on the leaves—how this one is different from that one, this finer than that. Or we can look to the one life of the tree. If we concentrate on differences, the whole is impossibly complex and confusing. As a boy, and now as a man, I badly need to understand the one life of the tree. This brings me the peace of heaven. I find myself in profound accord with a man born three centuries ago, a man who walked in silver buckled shoes and me in Adidas sneakers. He put words to what used to be nameless for me:

> IT IS PLAIN THAT THE CHURCH OF THE LORD IS NOT HERE, NOR THERE, BUT THAT IT IS EVERYWHERE, BOTH WITHIN THOSE KINGDOMS WHERE THE CHURCH IS, AND OUTSIDE THEM, WHERE MEN LIVE ACCORDING TO THE PRECEPTS OF CHARITY. HENCE IT IS THAT THE CHURCH OF THE LORD IS SCATTERED THROUGH THE WHOLE WORLD, AND YET IT IS ONE; FOR WHEN LIFE MAKES THE CHURCH AND NOT DOCTRINE SEPARATE FROM LIFE, THEN THE CHURCH IS ONE, BUT WHEN DOCTRINE MAKES THE CHURCH, THEN THERE ARE MANY.
>
> — *Arcana Coelestia* 8152

I have difficulty in answering the question of what religion I belong to. If the questioner is reflective I answer with surprise, "Do you

18. Wilson Van Dusen, *Uses: A Way of Personal and Spiritual Growth* (New York: Swedenborg Foundation, 1981).

honestly mean there is more than one?" But to others I answer simply, "I belong to all religions."

Some will think it must be a life of constant highs to be a mystic. Not so. Much of the time I grumble at my fate and God kicks me. It is sometimes that way with lovers. But it is a respite to wander among Swedenborg's words, touched here and there, and shot through with a wonderful light.

The Mystery of Ordinary Experiencing

THE EXTERNAL AFFECTIONS OF THOUGHT MANIFEST THEMSELVES IN BODILY SENSATION, AND SOMETIMES IN THE THOUGHT OF THE MIND, BUT THE INTERNAL AFFECTIONS OF THE THOUGHT FROM WHICH THE EXTERNAL EXIST NEVER MAKE THEMSELVES MANIFEST TO MAN. OF THESE HE KNOWS NO MORE THAN A RIDER ASLEEP IN A CARRIAGE DOES OF THE ROAD OR THAN ONE FEELS THE ROTATION OF THE EARTH. NOW, WHEN MAN KNOWS NOTHING OF THE THINGS BEYOND NUMBER THAT TAKE PLACE IN THE INTERIORS OF HIS MIND, AND THE FEW EXTERNAL THINGS WHICH COME TO THE SIGHT OF HIS THOUGHT . . . HOW CAN ANYONE ASSERT THAT ONE'S OWN PRUDENCE DOES ALL THINGS? WERE YOU TO SEE JUST ONE IDEA LAID OPEN, YOU WOULD SEE ASTOUNDING THINGS, MORE THAN TONGUE CAN TELL.

— Emanuel Swedenborg, *Divine Providence* 199

Let's see—I am puzzled what to say. My fingers are clamped over my mouth and I stare at the things in my study with a hard feeling of determination. My head feels hot, as it does when I'm concentrating. What am I to say about ordinary experiencing? I scan several notes scattered on my desk. Still the fingers clamped over my mouth and the feelings of hard determination. Bits of ideas come to consciousness. "Why not start out with—an example of ordinary experience? No. That moves too fast. It sweeps over a number of mysteries as though each was understood." I sit back in my chair and swallow. Now a single finger is clamped over my lips. "I'll have to do both—show the range of things, and then show how each is not fully comprehended."

The whole tenor of this experience was set by the felt need to write. The fingers *clamped* over my mouth was a spontaneous outward representation of my state. The tone of the state was hard, determined. Yet I did not know what to say. The hard gesture reflected the determination (clamped) as well as not knowing what to say (lips covered). Later, when I was more nearly ready to write, there was only one finger guarding the mouth. Staring at the things in the study, searching notes, and scanning ideas that came to me all had the same implications. My response to a felt problem (how to write of ordinary experience) was rapidly and spontaneously represented in a number of ways (hand on mouth, staring, searching notes, checking ideas coming to me, hot head, feeling of hard determination). What I could not see at first later emerged as a conflict in directions—whether to describe the whole flow of experience or to capture one bit of it accurately. The response to the conflict was to move back in my chair (association—sit back and take another look) and swallow (association—try to digest this). The resolving of two trends into one came as I clamped one finger over my mouth. The solution was to accept both trends as part of one.

What I have briefly described was an ordinary experience. The first thing to note is that it represents itself spontaneously and simultaneously on several levels at once—gesture, bodily sensations, inward feeling, actions taken, ideas emerging, self-reflection, and decision making. This in itself is quite remarkable. We are something that can represent itself in several ways simultaneously. This occurs whether we pay much attention to these ways or not. In fact, we often focus on one ("I wonder what I should say?") and hardly notice the other representations. In other words, though we exist on several levels simultaneously, we may choose to focus on one or more of these as the real, main, or only level.

This limiting of self to a single prominent level is done so commonly that many forget the greater complexity of experience. Because we explain ourselves in verbal terms, the verbal level has become preeminent. In the above instance, if asked "What are you doing?" I would have been inclined to answer "Just working on a problem." The verbal answer is coded shorthand for a complex process all of whose parts are not necessarily even known. The reliance on the verbal as the main or only level of internal processes leads some to think that thought is just unspoken words. Let us focus closer on them.

Phenomenology represents a serious effort to capture human experience just as it is. When the effort of phenomenology is focused on a tiny portion of human experience it acts like a psychological microscope. When I focus the microscope on the formation of words in my head, the bit I would choose is the sudden appearance of ideas. What is it really like when an idea becomes conscious enough that it can be said to myself internally, or externally spoken of?

"I am now formulating this sentence." I felt the general tenor of this sentence before I had finished writing the one before it. It felt like a simple declarative beginning—almost too simple, rather naked and alone. I began to hear it inwardly before it was set down. It was as though I were listening to someone speak. The tenor of the words was felt before they were said, the laying out of meaning was there before they were spoken in my head, and they were said in my head before they were written. These are like successive waves of clarification, each one running over the one before. The whole process took perhaps less than a second. The ending of the sentence also trailed off in a slightly scary feeling. It was as though the gap from the end of one sentence to the next was a little frightening until the next one came.

Focus your own phenomenological microscope on the simple process of thinking up a sentence. See if the process isn't something like the following:

There is a feeling of a need for something.

There is a background feeling it is coming.

The feeling becomes a presentiment of meaning.

The felt meaning germinates into internal speech.

The internal speech lays out a sentence—the end of which is felt while the first part is being heard.

If the sentence is to be spoken, the not-yet spoken parts are going through stages of being felt, emerging understanding, being heard, spoken.

After the sentence there is a trailing off of feeling, meaning, like an afterglow.

All this may seem like pedantic detailing. Yet it has profound implications. What I would normally think I thought up is really the result of a more complex growth of feelings into words. The feelings are mine, I guess. I have so little idea of their nature, structure, origin, or future directions that it is perhaps presumptuous to say they are mine. It might be more accurate to say I am theirs!

Furthermore, if we sort through the catalog of processes we have cleverly named as existing in people's experience, all of them stem from feeling.

Attitudes are a more or less permanent feeling toward things. This feeling-attitude tends to condition response. Action is preceded by feeling. We will see later in the hypnogogic state that feeling can be seen shaping words or images. Fantasy tells the story of feeling. Logical processes are a kind of guardedness and structuring of feeling. Memory is very much based on feeling.

It might help clarify the whole catalog of internal processes if they were seen as points in a continuum of differentiation. The vaguest feeling is the undifferentiated end of the continuum. Specific thoughts, words, memories, images, acts are the multiple outputs of the differentiated end of the continuum. These multiple outputs are related (words in my head are related to words said are related to acts, etc.). Essentially it is the underpinnings, the undifferentiated source of these end-products, that is more elusive to us. We more or less identify with the differentiated end-products. Some identify with these products to the exclusion of their feeling source. As we look closer at processes that primarily represent the life of feeling (fantasy, hypnogogic state, dreams), we have more difficulty identifying with this feeling base as our own making. When the feeling base handily spins off symbolic ideas and images it becomes even more difficult to name it as our own doing. Yet, if it is not fully our own doing, then neither are its products (our thoughts, actions, etc.).

The issue is where one will pin one's personal identity. What can one say "Yea, that is myself!" to? If I say "I make these words," then I must defend control over the whole feeling process underlying them. Yet we will see later that feeling can also speak symbolic ideas that few even understand! It is enough to indicate clearly at this juncture that the I—what I really call me-mine and take responsibility for—is best not limited yet. It is a fundamental issue. This is no minor, simple question. One fundamental answer that emerges from the study of many myths, religions, and one's own experience is: let the personal identity be everything and nothing simultaneously. When one carefully explores the boundaries of personal identity they expand beyond all expectations. The broadening of these boundaries may well be the root of wisdom.

When some feel the necessary humility of leaving open their identity, they feel to have a name, to say I, reflects a lack of wisdom. I can bear a name, and sign checks for convenience, and yet not feel bound by this punctilious boundary of self. The book has a cover and a definite title, and yet may talk of remote worlds. We are such books that we can be circumscribed by titles and yet understood as not circumscribed at all. The title is not the limitation, but the way we conceive of our self is.

A very simple and ordinary example that disturbs the conception of our boundaries is the way we are made up of our ancestors. One can conceive of one's hereditary parents and grandparents almost like curious assigned data or a social security number. Yet a careful examination of personal experience shows individuals to be at least partly shaped by their parents and significant others. The perceived parent, the one experienced and lived with, is introjected and woven into the fabric of one's experience. This is both the perceived parent and the real parent. Insofar as the mother is well perceived, it is more of the real mother that is introjected. The individual is also shaped around what the parents transmitted genetically. Beyond the obvious eye and hair color, and the like, we don't know how much of our psychic experience is involved in this transmission. An individual is also shaped in part by the cultural traditions and even subtle mores of the groups he has lived with. In view of this, it would be more accurate to say that, at least in part, we are the confluence of many others. All those "others" can never be fully catalogued. The confluence of their influences is part of the vast, unknown, undifferentiated background world of the individual. The differentiated individual is the resultant. We are coming under the influence of many others by our increasing participation in the media. How much we are shaped by the cultural matrices we exist in is only now becoming clear with the growth of anthropology and sociology.

However we split it, the boundaries of the self are relatively vast and unclear. But for appropriate convenience we set them at the skin. What is inside the skin is mine, outside it is other. Since I perceive and react to others and am really compounded of others in several ways, this skin boundary should be viewed as a useful fiction. It is the same as saying a book is bound by its covers. This is true enough if one wants to take the most limited view of the book, but it overlooks its contents, where they came from, and the effects they might have on the worlds of others.

The apparently simple issue of what is the boundary of the individual is best left open Any closing of it is an artificial limiting of our conception. The individual is at the confluence of heredity, parents, significant others, his culture, language, schooling, and the media. He is transcended by these, and in many real respects he is their resultant. When we look closely at the simplest of human experiences we find the so-called individual also transcended within by sensations he doesn't plan and by feelings that seem the general background and source of his experiencing. Consciousness is the running, moment-by-moment bit of clarity and awareness at the confluence of these forces. One's own words emerge out of a sea of feeling—meaning—presentiments. We are the meeting place of at least a number of transcendencies. The discovery of this should not be a matter of great pride or despair. It is just things as they are.

I once worked with a man in a legal experiment on the effects of the drug LSD. We were in a relatively barren hospital room. It took me a while to discover that the man was going around the room quietly naming things. "That is a chair," he would say to himself. Under LSD everything had become too lively and a little frightening. He pinned them down and limited their existence by naming them. He might as well have said, "You are *only* a chair." I fear our hanging an identity on the sequential confluence of transcendent experiences does about the same thing. Naming implies that we have comprehended, circumscribed, delimited, put down. Naming the chair doesn't mean I really understand how it is made or what it is. It says, in effect, you are of the class of things I've seen before. Of course self or personal identity is also of the class of things I've seen before—whatever it is!

But watch my fingers writing. Theoretically I know how they move. Brain to nerve to muscle, etc. Brilliant. I theoretically understand how I move! Yet secretly I don't really understand brain, nerve, or muscle. Practically speaking, do I know how I move? Well, let's see. I feel the finger pressing the pencil, moving it over the paper. The movements are very fast, but barely able to keep up with inner speech. I pause a moment, resting the hand, watching to see what else will come out of inner speech. I seem to be just this sequence of experiences: feeling, to inner speech, to finger movements. I am this coming together, whatever it is! This confluence seems to be conscious of the meeting. The confluence of experiencing is consciousness. I am the confluence that is consciousness that is experiencing what is here. Yet when this consciousness examines in detail any aspect of its experience it does not fully comprehend or rule it.

Our experience has flowing into it more than we generally understand. It is the same with our body. Though we live in it, move it, and indeed are it, we don't fully understand a single organ of it, nor in deed a single cell. Whatever this experiencing is called, it is only beginning to open up the nature of its experience because it is transcended at every hand. Though it can name experiencing or consciousness, these too it does not understand.

If you have followed my arguments, you may have several possible reactions.

1. You can't really see that anything transcends you. In which case I would charge you to examine fully a single thought as it emerges. If your thoughts are too fast for you, try to slow them down, and examine several hundred of them. If you get handy at that, then examine examining. Tiring of that, try to hold one thought in mind for five minutes and record all the places your mind wandered off to and try to see the blanknesses that precede wandering.

2. You are puzzled that I seem to call into question conventional ideas of the boundary of personal identity. It will not be nearly so difficult or threatening to explore the further operations of mind if boundaries of self are left open.

3. You feel bothered, or better yet crushed, by the idea that you are transcended at every quarter. One becomes accustomed to this, and like open boundaries, it removes impediments.

So much for very ordinary experience that represents itself and exists on many levels, in many ways easily and spontaneously—whatever IT is.

Reincarnation: The Universal Return

Most people believe reincarnation means that the individual returns again to this world. I will show this to be an idea that, although inaccurate and illusory itself, points toward the real truth: God, the Universal, returns endlessly.

There are actually two doctrines of reincarnation. The simpler one, known to most everyone, is that the individual returns again to this world. I shall refer to this as the lesser doctrine. The other doctrine is that ultimately there really is no individual, and that God alone reappears endlessly through the whole of creation. I'll call this the greater doctrine. The greater one is less widely known, and it is the more difficult to understand. The major religions that deal with reincarnation are Hinduism and Buddhism, though aspects of it can be found in almost all religions, including Christianity.[1] The tendency in the West is to emphasize the supremacy of the individual. Corresponding to this the Western tendency is to be aware of only the lesser doctrine. Countless Western authors, including many followers of Swedenborg, have rejected the possibility of the individual returning.

---

1. Head, J., and Cranston, S. L. *Reincarnation, an East-West Anthology*. Wheaton, IL, Theosophical Publishing House, 1961.

This has created the appearance of a split between Christianity and the oriental religions on this matter. The split is unfortunate and unnecessary since even in the oriental religions the lesser doctrine is only part of a beneficial illusion. Christianity, Swedenborg and the oriental religions basically support the greater doctrine. Indeed some of the clearest statements on the greater doctrine are to be found in Swedenborg. But first let us look more closely at the lesser doctrine.

Many treat religion as an organized body of ideas passed from one to another. I personally believe there are experiential roots to religion. If we could suddenly wipe out all doctrinal teachings, I believe, in time, people would return to much the same ideas because they arise from their experience. What are the possible experiential roots to the idea that we might return again to this world? For one it is *the only world* many know. Spiritual worlds seem very theoretical to most people. "This world is it. If I must die, I'd like to come back to this world."

But there is a deeper root to this idea. I, like many, have simply looked around the animal kingdom and fantasized which animal I'd like to be. I don't want to come back as a tiger and have to catch and kill my food. I'd like to be a sea gull, watch ships come and go, soar in the air, walk on land and even explore under water. Psychologists have made use of this tendency for us to become others. They ask what animal you would like to be and then explore the aspect of you that is reflected in the animal's way of living. I rescued an infant squirrel and raised it by hand, and now I feel kin to squirrels. In a word, I am speaking of empathy. Mothers feel the lives of their children and suffer through their children's troubles. This normal empathetic tendency to slip into other lives is one of the roots of the lesser reincarnation. This empathy is very useful. It leads to concern for the welfare of others, love, understanding and peace. It leads in the direction of mankind's highest ideals. It is reflected in the Golden Rule, which is at the center of Christianity, Buddhism, and other religions. Empathy is a positive exercise and so socially valuable it should be deliberately cultivated. It is, I believe, one of the experiential roots of the idea of reincarnation. For some, empathy goes back in history. My wife and I walked in a ruined abbey, and we both felt the peaceful, workaday lives of the monks who had lived there centuries before. For others empathy flashes forward in time, and they feel the harm man is doing to Mother Earth for future generations.

There is another experience that leads more directly to the idea of the lesser reincarnation. People occasionally actually experience a past life. There are examples all the way from the vague to the specific and confirmable. The best examples I know of are in the journals of the American and British Societies for Psychical Research. In a few instances the past life that was recalled could be confirmed in considerable detail. My guess is that the most substantial and confirmable cases of recalling a past life have occurred in countries such as India, where the idea of reincarnation is generally accepted. I myself once had an intimation of having lived before. I had a headache, and a fellow psychologist suggested that I explore my associations with the pain to see what I would find. I discovered an intense awareness of the life of a Mayan priest. I'll not burden you with the details, but this intense recall of my life as a Mayan priest faded only gradually after a period of months. These experiences force us to consider the possibility that we really have lived before.

I also found examples of the experience of past lives while doing clinical trials with LSD. Several clients spontaneously recalled either one past life or a whole series of past lives. I had pretty much rejected the ideas of reincarnation as a foolish notion until I saw intelligent people, with no knowledge of or belief in reincarnation, stumbling onto past lives. My religious understanding is really governed by what I find. And when I find what was totally unexpected I look closer. In each instance the past life was like an image in great depth and detail reflecting the present person. I am convinced that even if the whole idea of reincarnation is totally false, it would still be useful to a person to experience a past life. There was an odd detail in the first case I came across. The subject was an alcoholic woman noted for a life of infidelities. She discovered she had lived as a Bavarian woman whose husband had died young. In her past life she had remained faithful to her husband's memory, and only repented her constancy on her deathbed, when she vowed never to waste a lifetime in fidelity again.

So in this case the past life was a direct opposite of the present life. In my own case, whether or not I ever lived before as a particular Mayan priest, the life of this priest is a more accurate representation of my present religious life than any I might devise. Clearly past lives are not happenstance. I can only become aware of a past life that is intimately related to me. I have had occultists glibly tell me of my own past lives, and they meant little to me. I could not feel their validity. But my life and that of the Mayan priest are intimately interlinked.

Let me briefly look at the doctrine of karma, which is a partner to the idea of reincarnation. Karma says that what I do to others, I receive back. It is related to the Golden Rule or spiritual justice. Karma refers to the very nature of events. What I do to others is done to me. But as he looks about him, the individual doesn't always see spiritual justice. This is perhaps another experience leading to the idea of reincarnation. Perhaps if I don't see someone getting his just desserts in this life, then he will in future lives. So we can accumulate karma in this life and get it back later. As a good Hindu I look at a dictator who bleeds a country dry to fatten Swiss bank accounts and I think, I would not want his karma, for all his wealth. The harm he has done could take countless lives to undo. No matter how poor my life, insofar as I believe in God and do my best, I prefer my own karma. This postponement of pain or benefit is also common in Christianity, but it occurs in the next spiritual world rather than in future lives in this world.

I see the idea of karma as so useful I'd be the last to want to disturb it. It says there is profound justice in existence, even if you can't see it. Personally I see much justice though it is often subtle. If I rape women and get away with it, I am *already paying*—I don't know love. I live a terrible, furtive existence, fearing the next knock on the door is the police. There is justice if you look for it. We would like the assaulter assaulted. But I fear karmic justice is even more internal, more spiritual, and even more just.

In the West we are inclined to throw out karma because of its association with "countless lives," the lesser reincarnation. But perhaps we haven't looked closely enough. In the Hindu-Buddhist thesis, it is possible to get off the wheel of endless lives and endless making up for karma, and finally come to a heaven beyond this world. How? By coming to realize the ultimate truth that only God exists. It isn't enough to mouth this truth. It must pervade your very existence. In effect, it is being trapped in the idea of the little self as the be-all and end-all of existence that leads to countless lives and the endless working off of karma. Swedenborg's *proprium*, being for myself alone, fits here. Being for myself alone I am caught in conflict with others and remain in the endless working off of karma in reincarnation. The opposite, being for others, leads towards empathy, love and release. Full release comes when I see that ego is empty and that ultimately only God exists. God endlessly reenters creation as this and that and all there is. Seeing this I am kind to all life, myself included. In this spirit some Buddhists try to avoid harm even to insects and bacteria. To my knowledge, unlike warlike Christianity, Buddhism has never been involved in warlike aggression. The person who senses the Universal in all things naturally follows the Golden Rule. In this view the statement "What you do to the least of these you do to me" (Matthew 25:40) is completely true. This discussion of the escape from karma has led us to the greater doctrine of reincarnation. It says indeed there is an endless return of life, but that it is ultimately only God's life that returns.

Under laboratory conditions I have experimented with altered states of consciousness in individuals. We didn't suggest these states. We just altered brain chemistry and looked to see what would happen. The experiments I refer to here were all undertaken with gifted normals, mostly advanced psychology students. I had several subjects who spent the whole day working back through many past lives. I recall particularly one young woman who worked back through animal lives to primeval ooze. She broke through this to a tremendous vision of the Divine. After about the third subject who did this, I recalled that this is something like Buddha's own experience working back through past lives to the experience of God. It was as though a puzzle were being undone. At first it seemed to the subjects that *they* had lived many lives before. But when the puzzle was solved it became completely apparent that only God existed and that it was God who had manifested in countless lives, including the current one. This is the greater doctrine.

Here is another way of describing what happens. I had some subjects who went easily and directly into the experience of God. The other subjects, who went through repeated incarnations, seemed to need a progressive loosening and expansion of ego boundaries before they could come to the experience of God. Expansion is the key idea here. It was not as though personal ego was destroyed. Personal identity remained throughout. But the understanding of what the person really was expanded until there was only the All. From this I concluded that the experience of reincarnation is *one* of the avenues to enlightenment. This was the experience that led me to suspect there was also a greater doctrine of reincarnation. I later amply confirmed it by consulting with a Buddhist priest and Buddhist and Hindu texts in translation. It is fundamental in these texts that ego is an illusion, the mask of Brahma who is the God over all. An illusion doesn't reincarnate, not in any real sense. But an illusion can have the appearance of reincarnation (the lesser doctrine) until God is known (escaping from the wheel of lives, the greater doctrine). The very fact that it is possible to end the apparent reincarnation of the individual points to the fact that it is fundamentally an illusion. It *seems* the individual returns until God's role is seen and the illusion disappears.

Only recently did I begin to examine the uses of the lesser reincarnation/karma combination. It was immediately apparent that avoiding inexorable karma means leading life in accordance with the Golden Rule, which even Christ described as the essence of the Bible. But then I saw that even the act of considering what my past lives were, or might be in the future, links me with others. The tendency of taking past lives seriously is towards the One Life. How is it that what I do unto you will be done unto me? Only insofar as we are both of God and in God. Then surely what is done returns to itself. I detect in much western writing on reincarnation that people who know of the greater doctrine are teaching the lesser one because its general tendency is in a useful spiritual direction. Consideration of past lives and possible future ones is similar to my subjects going through a loosening up of ego boundaries.

It seems strange to me that I have not seen anyone link the idea of reincarnation to empathy. As I have noted, a person's empathy can extend back to what it was like to live before. Archaeologists have this empathy and so do collectors of antiques. Or empathy can extend forward toward future lives, as in the case of environmentalists and those concerned about ending wars. Or empathy can extend out in the present and include as part of one's very life children, friends, animals, and plants. It is almost as though we are fashioned to be more than just for ourselves alone. This takes reincarnation out of the realm of the strange and alien. Do you want to explore other lives? There are countless opportunities at hand. Here comes a stranger, a totally new life. Explore what this life is like.

The Buddhists use the analogy of a candle to explain reincarnation. I have an unlit candle that gives no light. It is lit by the One Flame that can light all candles. The candle is the body, individuality, the personal history. The One Flame that gives light is God. But burning here and lighting my study, it appears alone, unique. Reincarnation is a new candle lit by the old flame, the Universal. This is very similar to Swedenborg's statements that we are recipient vessels. The new vessel (candle) receives the influx (Universal Light). The quality of the vessel affects how well it reflects the light. The real mystery is, how could *I* experience the life of a long dead Mayan priest? Not because *I* am something, but because It, the Light, knows all lives. I was shown something of the Universal in my life that illuminates all human nature. We are essentially recipient vessels and ultimately what is received is the Universal. The journey from the individual to the Universal is a loosening and expansion of the boundaries of personhood. And it is also an intensification of personhood into its source and life, the Universal. Reincarnation and its companion doctrine of karma are both small aspects of this underlying drift towards the oneness of things.

The turning point between the lesser and greater doctrines of reincarnation really rests on the concept of what is the self. If you see the self as an independent, self-contained entity, then you will favor the lesser doctrine. Let us examine this supposedly self-sufficient self to see if it is so simply delimited. On the bodily level we seem to have a perfect picture of the limited self, bounded by the skin and thereby separate from all else. But wait a moment. If I take all the oxygen out of the room, the skin turns blue, and, given a few days, falls apart. Our skin selves are dependent on the gaseous atmosphere. Our skin selves are also dependent on what we eat, and on our habits and activities. Suppose my skin self lives with a group of people determined to keep me awake. In a few days I'll begin to go out of my mind and hallucinate, for I am dependent on what others permit. My skin self also reflects tension and the stress of my job or my relationships with others. So even on this most basic physical level, I am dependent on others and the environment. We begin to suspect the concept of a neatly packaged self is partly an illusion.

Can I really assess what you are without assessing your relationships? This lady is a mother with a nursing infant. We'd better consider them together. Another one is a man with wife and children dependent on him. Can we fully understand him without these relationships? If you want to know me you had better come see where I live and meet the other people whose lives touch mine. Even in a legal sense we are in the midst of a network of written contracts, such as marriage and property, and implied contracts—for instance, that we will drive our cars according to law.

If you really want to know me, you had better discover all my relationships. Even the language we speak puts us in a vast network of cultural history and understanding. I don't have the primitive's conception of time because it wasn't given me in my language. On the social level, where we humans exist, the idea of a neat, isolated, package self is really a profound illusion. It is a theoretical entity. In reality it doesn't even begin to exist. In reality what we are is spread out all over the place and impossible to delimit.

Now let us look at the situation theologically. I will use the theology of Swedenborg to lead into the Hindu-Buddhist greater doctrine of reincarnation. Why? Very simply because taking away some of the historical trappings of language, they deal with the same thing. We are still asking, "What is the self?" and this time answering with Swedenborg's theology. The trend we saw developing in the skin self and the social self continues at the theological level. We saw that the self is dependent on the environment and lives in a network of relationships. The idea that we are totally separate is fundamentally an illusion and is actually a very poor way of conceiving of humanness.

Swedenborg indicates that each person is associated with two spirits of hell and two of heaven. I'm not sure of the exactness of this count, but this reflects that we are in the confluence of the forces of heaven and hell. Insofar as we conceive of our self as a package self separate from and independent of all else, we drift towards hell. Hell is the ultimate of separateness. It also includes the idea that because we are separate we can do as we please because even if we hurt others we do not hurt ourselves.

Heaven is the opposite. I exist out of the will of God, which comes through the heavens and enters me as influx. Part of influx is that we are given to feel we control ourselves and are separate from others. But Swedenborg penetrated this appearance of separation and experienced the higher worlds of which everyone is a part. By our choices and innermost tendencies we are already part of a kingdom of heaven. A man's very thoughts and affections "reach out round about into heaven in keeping with its form, communicating marvelously with the communities there, and they in turn with him."[2] We are given into life and experience from the will of God, this life passing through the spiritual worlds into ourselves. Again we see we are dependent. Swedenborg says that if the will of God is withdrawn we are instantly dead. We are also networked. Spirits are with us. We are already becoming a part of a kingdom of heaven. The whole focus of religion is understanding and working with this spiritual interdependence and networking, which is our relationship to God. On the smallest level I am totally convinced influx not only occurs but it can be observed.[3] The recent blossoming

---

2. Swedenborg, E. *Heaven and Hell.* No. 203. New York, Swedenborg Foundation, 1979.
3. Van Dusen, W. *The Natural Depth in Man.* Chs. 6–7. New York, Swedenborg Foundation, 1981.

of evidence of near-death experiences suggests that whatever we are, we continue beyond the life of the body.[4]

The center of Swedenborg's works is the process of regeneration. The most detailed treatment of it is in his twelve-volume *Arcana Coelestia* [Heavenly Secrets]. In regeneration we move from the conception of the unitary spiritual self into the more heavenly world of usefulness and networking towards the experience of God.[5] I think one of the most pervasive errors in theology is that many think moving from awareness of self to awareness of God must represent a loss of self. I can only say the experience is far from loss.

> THE MORE CLOSELY ONE IS CONJOINED TO THE LORD THE MORE DISTINCTLY DOES HE SEEM TO HIMSELF TO BE HIS OWN, AND THE MORE PLAINLY DOES HE RECOGNIZE THAT HE IS THE LORD'S.
>
> — Swedenborg, *Divine Providence* 42

The idea of loss of self is rooted in the idea of the unitary package of self. It never did exist. It is illusion on whatever level you examine it. The experience of moving from self-awareness into the full awareness of God is a continuous one of expansion of the self. Not loss, but expansion. Finally the expansion reveals the ultimate truth. Only God exists. What was called the self before was the life of God hidden in darkness.

> FROM MUCH EXPERIENCE I HAVE COME TO KNOW THAT THERE IS BUT ONE LIFE—THE LORD'S.
>
> — Swedenborg, *Arcana Coelestia* 3484

This is the greater doctrine of the Hindu-Buddhist reincarnation. What really lives keeps turning up endlessly. You are that One Life. Or

4. Ring, K. *Life at Death*, New York, Quill, 1982.

5. Van Dusen, W. *Uses: A Way of Personal and Spiritual Growth*. New York, Swedenborg Foundation, 1981.

as the Hindus say, *Tat tuam asi'*, that thou art. Awareness of the One Life ends the endless round of rebirth again into a struggling skin, trying to figure out what it is. The struggle of you versus others ends in the discovery of the One that is the All. In the Hindu-Buddhist concept this ends maya, the illusion of the isolated, package self. Regeneration expands the self into a total relationship with and interdependence with others, called heaven. And the ultimate understanding of the celestial angels of heaven is that only God exists. Was the self lost in the process? Decidedly not. It discovered itself everywhere, until it found All there is.

You might wonder, why speak at all of reincarnation and karma if they simply lead toward the great understanding that is dealt with in other ways in Christianity? I think the usefulness of the idea can be seen at the small level of the lesser doctrine. The person considering reincarnation looks to see if his life is somehow connected to lives that went before and will come after. Indeed it is. This is one way to begin the expansion of the concept of the self. But we see the real power of the idea is not in the self coming back, but in beginning to identify with what always was and always will be. When this identification is complete, the lesser doctrine fades and the greater doctrine is seen as the real truth. I think anything that undoes that illusion of the separate, isolated self is useful. I hope my readers can begin to see themselves as existing in a complex and not totally definable network of relations and interdependencies. You might try fantasizing about how you lived before. Or look around you and see what different lives and forms of life you can identify with. I easily become a sea gull. Big, with an awkward waddle on land, but smooth in the heavens. I enjoy sitting on pilings and watching ships and people come and go. This is a new freedom, a freedom to be anyone, or anything, in any time.

You might wonder if I still think I was that Mayan priest. Indeed yes. His struggle to know God was as much mine as anything could possibly be. I identify with his purpose, which continues today with me. The trick here is in allowing the self to be enlarged, rather than clinging to the illusion of the little, cut-off self. And this is the turning point between the lesser and the greater doctrine of reincarnation. And it also leads in the direction of understanding the perfect unity of it all.

"So do I come back into this world to suffer the karma of all I've done?" Indeed yes. You are the one who returns endlessly. In this way I pay homage to the lesser doctrines of reincarnation and karma. They are very, very true, but not in the way usually conceived.

The Soul, Hidden and Manifest

In this paradoxical title I have condensed the whole sweep of Swedenborg's search for the soul. He began with a conception of the soul that was abstract and hidden. He used the soul much as we do now as the essence of the human, an essence so abstract and philosophical that the idea is of doubtful utility. But Swedenborg's quest for the soul was more persistent and thoroughgoing than most, and he eventually found it in aspects of the human that are relatively obvious and manifest. So much so that I will attempt to describe some features of souls I know! But first let us begin where he began, and in the sequence in which he found it; we'll gradually discover the obvious and manifest soul.

If you pull together all Swedenborg's references to the soul, a clear pattern emerges. In the period prior to his introduction into the spiritual world in 1743, he makes frequent reference to the soul. After his entry into the spiritual world, there are relatively few references to the soul. Something had happened. Prior to ever seeing and dealing with souls in the spiritual world, the concept was relatively abstract and slippery to deal with. After his introduction into the spiritual world, the concept became much clearer and more concrete as the spiritual self. It would be somewhat tedious and unnecessary to catalog all the changes in his idea of the soul before he ever saw one. The important thing is the nature and direction of his quest for the soul.

When I looked at the current dictionary definition of the soul, it surprised me that it is still very representative of his pre-enlightenment conception of what he was looking for.

> Soul. 1. The principle of life, feeling thought, and action in man, regarded as a distinct entity separate from the body, and commonly held to be separable in existence from the body; the spiritual part as distinct from the physical part. 2. The spiritual part of man regarded in its moral aspect, or as believed to survive death and be subject to happiness or misery in a life to come: arguing for the immorality of the soul . . . 4. The emotional part of a man's nature; the seat of the feelings or sentiments. 5. A human being; person. . . . 7. The animating principle; the essential element or part of something.[1]

This is what Swedenborg spent some years looking for. His conception essentially lay on the border of God and man. Though a person *is* a soul, one could not really say he possessed a soul, as one would possess a suit of clothes. The soul is the very essential of life. It was made by God, and in some respects it is the temple of God within the individual. So it partakes of both God and man. Swedenborg's search for the soul prior to his enlightenment was then a search for God and the essence of the human at the same time. In view of the scope of what he wanted and later achieved, I'd have to say that he was on target in conceiving of his essential quest as a search for the soul. His interest was really both God and person, and how these interrelate.

The extent and seriousness of his quest is a little hard to grasp. It is seen in part if one stacks up all the volumes written between the 1734 *Mechanism of the Soul and Body* and the 1745 *Worship and Love of God*. This includes his basic anatomical works. He went into anatomy because the soul fashions an appropriate temple for itself in the body.

1. *The Random House Dictionary of the English Language*, Random House, N.Y.C., 1966.

In all the internal functions of the body, and in its senses and movement capacity, the soul has expressed itself. Perhaps by examining this temple that reflects its nature, something of the soul could be seen. This period also includes his major philosophical works, for philosophy was the use of reason to try to reconstruct the nature of the soul. The principal volumes which contain both an anatomical and a philosophical approach to the soul were titled by the translator, *The Economy of the Animal Kingdom*. It was mistitled. A better recent translation is *Dynamics of the Soul's Domain*. In effect, his work in anatomy was a first foray into the Soul's Kingdom. He had come from the physical sciences, and his first approach was through the physical. He did acquire a broad and, at the same time, a more concrete understanding of the soul by this venture into anatomy. This spiritual understanding of the physical body was to remain with him all his life and shows later in the concept of the Grand Man. He was ahead of his time. He would easily appreciate our current psychosomatic understanding.[2] Later he spoke of his venture into anatomy as though he had perhaps gone too far, where few readers could follow him. "But thus far I have felt bound to venture, for I have resolved, cost what it may, to trace out the nature of the human soul."[3]

But, in effect, he was working a dry hole. He very aptly described what was wrong.

ON A SLIGHT CONSIDERATION OF THE SUBJECT, I COULD NOT BUT THINK WITH MANKIND IN GENERAL, THAT ALL OUR KNOWLEDGE OF [THE SOUL] WAS TO BE ATTEMPTED EITHER BY A BARE REASONING PHILOSOPHY, OR MORE IMMEDIATELY BY THE ANATOMY OF THE HUMAN BODY. BUT UPON MAKING THE ATTEMPT, I FOUND MYSELF AS FAR FROM MY OBJECT AS EVER; FOR NO SOONER DID I SEEM TO HAVE MASTERED THE SUBJECT, THEN I FOUND IT AGAIN ELUDING MY GRASP, THOUGH IT NEVER ABSOLUTELY DISAPPEARED FROM MY

2. Van Dusen, W. "Modern Findings on Swedenborg's Correspondence," in *God-Man Communication*, Swedenborg Foundation, N.Y.C., 1982.

3. Swedenborg, E. *Economy of the Animal Kingdom*, Part 2, n. 214, New Church Press, N.Y.C., 1955.

VIEW. THUS MY HOPES WERE NOT DESTROYED, BUT DEFERRED; AND I FREQUENTLY REPROACHED MYSELF WITH STUPIDITY IN BEING IGNORANT OF THAT WHICH WAS YET EVERYWHERE MOST REALLY PRESENT TO ME; SINCE BY REASON OF THE SOUL IT IS THAT WE HEAR, SEE, FEEL, PERCEIVE, REMEMBER, IMAGINE, THINK, DESIRE, WILL; OR THAT WE ARE, MOVE, AND LIVE.

— Swedenborg, *Economy of the Animal Kingdom*, Part 2, n. 208

In a few words, he was after the very basis of all human experience. It is fortunate that he didn't make the common mistake of assuming, once we grasp brain, we also understand mind. For mind and brain are such different realms, and we are still, two centuries later, hard put to describe how they interact. Swedenborg also surveyed the best of the world's wisdom literature on the soul. This is in his *Philosopher's Note Book*. How else can we proceed beyond these approaches? He then chose to look at mental functioning itself to find the soul. This was a bit of genius because he was in an age that used philosophical reason to speculate on the faculties of mind. He did this too, in part, but he also brought in a good measure of direct experience. He meditated, and this practice reflected in his work.[4] Hence was born his *Rational Psychology*. The original manuscript for this was untitled and was part of the *Regnum Animale* (The Soul's Kingdom). His *Psychology* was once appropriately titled *The Soul or Rational Psychology*. This work partakes both of philosophical reasoning and human experience. The real significance of this period was that he had finally left behind the physical and was now looking directly at human experience. The significance of this might not be apparent, but the shift from philosophical speculation on mind to looking at mental experience itself had taken centuries. He had left behind the benchmarks of the wisdom literature on the soul and the nervous system. He was opening new territory with only God to guide him. This was the period in which he was turning from being a physical scientist to a spiritual seer.

If you just looked at three of the works produced in this time, you could see big things coming. In 1743–1744 he wrote and did not

4. Van Dusen, W. "Meditation," in *New Philosophy*, Dec. 1975, p. 309–322.

publish his very private *Journal of Dreams*. Here was the soul's own peculiar language. He easily penetrated it and began to see into all things symbolic. His later Doctrine of Correspondences really dates from his work on dreams. The soul speaks this spontaneous and natural spiritual language in dreams. He could decode the message.

The next volume was *The Messiah About To Come*. This was, like the *Dreams*, an unpublished private journal. I have commented at length on this pivotal work elsewhere.[5] Basically he prayed to know God directly. In this book he recorded Biblical passages which spoke to him. The central theme was about the coming of the Messiah into his life. In a dramatic final line, God came and wrote through his hand on what was to be the essence of Swedenborg's life. It is strange Swedenborg scholars missed the importance of this gem.

The third volume of this period was one of his strangest and most beautiful works. That it would be done was predicted by his soul and earlier recorded in the *Journal of Dreams*. Here is how he had to proceed earlier.

> THEREFORE THAT I MAY EXPLORE THE SOUL, IT IS NECESSARY THAT I UNFOLD THOSE MANIFOLD COVERINGS WHICH REMOVE HER FROM OUR EYES AS THOUGH SHE DWELT IN SOME CENTER. I MUST PROCEED BY THE ANALYTIC WAY, OR THROUGH EXPERIENCE TO CAUSES, AND THEN THROUGH CAUSES TO PRINCIPLES; THAT IS TO SAY FROM POSTERIOR THINGS TO PRIOR. SUCH IS THE ONLY WAY TO KNOWLEDGE OF THINGS SUPERIOR THAT IS GRANTED US. AND WHEN BY THIS WAY WE HAVE BEEN RAISED UP TO GENUINE PRINCIPLES, THEN FIRST IT IS PERMITTED US TO PROCEED BY THE SYNTHETIC WAY, THAT IS TO SAY, FROM PRIOR TO THINGS POSTERIOR. THIS IS THE WAY OF THE SOUL IN HER ACTION UPON THE BODY.
>
> — Swedenborg, *Rational Psychology*, Preface

In *The Worship and Love of God* he allows himself the freedom to describe the creation of the soul by God and how the soul creates its

5. Swedenborg, E. *The Messiah About to Come*, Academy of the New Church, Bryn Athyn, Penn., 1949.

body and lives through it. It is a dramatic, lovely and imaginative work totally out of character for Swedenborg. The scene is in the Garden of Eden. The focus is on seeing everything from the viewpoint of Adam's soul. It is a dramatic presentation of the life of the soul, in which he could finally go from prior things to posterior. If I were asked where does Swedenborg best describe the soul and its life, I would have to say it is in this volume. Here he isn't laboring with anatomical details and philosophical abstractions. He lays it all out from God, through soul and man, into the world. His later comments suggest he was uncomfortable with this book. But I am not. The soul's language in dreams is colorful and dramatic. Why not describe it in a language the soul is comfortable with?! A few quotes will give the flavor of this unusual book.

> THE SOUL, BURNING WITH THIS DESIRE, AS A MIND FORMED TO THE IMAGE OF THE SUPREME MIND, BEGAN ALSO TO BUILD A KIND OF LITTLE WORLD OR MICROCOSM AFTER THE EFFIGY OF THE GREAT WORLD, BUT NOT OUT OF NOTHING, WITH THE ETERNAL PURPOSE OF CLOTHING HERSELF WITH IT AS A BODY, AND THAT SHE MIGHT OPERATE IN IT AS A KIND OF DEITY, ADMINISTERING LAWS AT PLEASURE BY MEANS OF THE UNDERSTANDING, AND SO HOLDING THE REINS OF HER NATURE ACCORDING TO HER INTUITIONS THAT SHE MIGHT HAVE ONLY TO REGARD ENDS . . .
>
> — Swedenborg, *The Worship and Love of God* 35

This, to me, is wonderfully suggestive. The soul is formed in the image of the Supreme Mind. As such it forms the body as a ruler in a microcosm. This soul is a she, even though this is the soul of Adam. And it is very curious she only has regard toward ends, as God might. This reminds me of the fact that the internal of a person has odd attributes, which we can barely describe. One is that it seems to think transtemporally, as though it partakes of eternity. More, from the same.

> THUS LIVED WHOLLY AND ENTIRELY THE SOUL, UNDER THE IMAGE OF AN INFANT CLOTHED WITH A BODY; FOR THE SOUL SAW THE BEAUTIES OF PARADISE SHINE THROUGH, AS IT WERE, HER OWN EYES, NOT HIS, AND DELIGHTED HERSELF NOT FROM THE HARMONIES OF EFFECTS, BUT FROM THE JOY OF USES, AND OF THE GOODNESS CONTEMPLATED IN THEM.
>
> — Swedenborg, *The Worship and Love of God* 43.2

Some would argue Adam was a special case, but my guess is that Swedenborg intends this as a fitting description of everyone's soul. I'm not sure why the soul is feminine but it seems fitting. In Jung's analytical psychology, the man's soul is feminine and the woman's is masculine, so each person is a microcosm containing all attributes. Note she sees beyond the things of the moment to uses and their goodness.

In this last quote, Swedenborg settles who finally acts in the soul.

> BUT ALL THESE THINGS WERE DONE UNDER THE INFLUENCE OF THE SUPREME DEITY PROVIDING, YEA ACTING, WHO IN ALL AND SINGLE THINGS IS THE SOLE AGENT, BECAUSE THE SOLE LIVING BEING; FOR FROM HIM, BECAUSE FROM HIS LIFE, WE LIVE, AND LIVING, ACT.
>
> — Swedenborg, *The Worship and Love of God* 43.3

Ultimately only God acts in creation. Later the soul detected aspects of herself that tended to earth, while she aspired upward. So the soul formed the mind to deal with this earthly aspect. This was published in 1745. Swedenborg has already been introduced into the spiritual world. It's a period of spiritual learning and change for him. He is studying the *Bible*. It is to be four years before volume one of the great *Arcana Coelestia* is to appear. I think the style of *Worship and Love of God* was a practice in freedom of expression where, for once, he could say how he felt the soul lived. It is also a period in which this great intellect was to discover and make good use of feeling. Abstract, tortuous philosophy was behind him now. In a sense, he was becoming more like the feelingful soul herself who sees ends and delights in the goodness of uses.

The Period of Enlightenment

Though the search for the soul was the central thrust of the more than 10 years of search preceding his enlightenment, the subject of the soul is small in his theological writings. In Potts giant 6 volume *Concordance,*[6] the soul takes up a mere 11 pages of over 5000 pages of references, or less than 0.002%. Why? Did he lose interest? No. I think the real answer is that he found the soul in such familiar terms that it now was treated under many headings. For instance, the soul was nothing else but the essential person, the spirit that lives on after death, and this is treated extensively in *Heaven and Hell*. Also, he had always used soul to mean the essential essence and inner life of a thing. He had found the soul of the Bible in its inner sense. This sense became a large part of all his writings after enlightenment.

> . . . FOR IN THE INTERNAL SENSE IS THE WORD'S SOUL OR LIFE, WHICH DOES NOT BECOME MANIFEST UNLESS THE SENSE OF THE LETTER AS IT WERE VANISHES — *Arcana Coelestia* 1405

One of Swedenborg's *Memorable Relations* best tells us what he now understands the soul to be. His *Memorable Relations* are spiritual events he experienced, which he tells us to convey a point. While in heaven, Swedenborg saw clouds that appeared to be full of contending swords of light. Beneath this was a marble training center in which young men were asked questions by a headmaster, beneath the gaze of assembled spirits and angels. The question was, "What is the soul, and what is its nature?" As each youth came up to answer, each put on a silk tunic of opaline color, and over it a gown of soft wool embroidered with flowers, and a cap with an ornament of roses encircled with sapphires. Each

6. Potts, J. *The Swedenborg Concordance*, Swedenborg Society, London, 1898, 6 vols.

youth in turn said that the soul is a mystery, but the first located it in the pineal gland, the second in the ventricles of the brain, the third in the heart. The fourth did better, saying the soul was a spiritual substance in the whole and in every part of man and is his life. The fifth gave the ancient view that the soul is like the breath that is breathed out as one dies. None of the youths' answers were satisfactory, so the audience prevailed on the principal to speak. Finally we have the heavenly answer.

> THE SOUL IS . . . A FORM, . . . IT IS THE FORM OF ALL THINGS OF LOVE AND OF ALL THINGS OF WISDOM; AND ALL THINGS OF LOVE ARE CALLED AFFECTIONS, AND ALL THINGS OF WISDOM ARE CALLED PERCEPTION. YOU ARE CALLED SPIRITS AND ANGELS . . . BUT NOW YOU SEE CLEARLY THAT YOU ARE IN TRUTH REALLY AND ACTUALLY MEN . . . YOU NOW KNOW THAT IT IS NOT THE MATERIAL BODY THAT LIVES AND THINKS, BUT A SPIRITUAL SUBSTANCE IN THE BODY; AND THIS YOU CALLED SOUL, WHOSE FORM YOU DID NOT KNOW, BUT WHICH YOU HAVE NOW SEEN AND CONTINUE TO SEE. . . .BECAUSE YOU ARE FORMS OF LOVE AND WISDOM FROM GOD, YOU CAN NEVER DIE. . . . IN A WORD THE SOUL IS THE MAN HIMSELF; FOR IT IS THE INMOST MAN, AND THEREFORE ITS FORM IS FULLY AND PERFECTLY THE HUMAN FORM. NEVERTHELESS, IT IS NOT LIFE, BUT THE RECEPTACLE OF LIFE FROM GOD NEAREST TO HIM, AND THUS GOD'S DWELLING PLACE. — *True Christian Religion* 697

Outside the marble hall Swedenborg saw that the contending swords of light had ended. There was a bright cloud whose light penetrated the roof and lit up the walls.

> AND I HEARD THAT WRITINGS WERE SEEN, AMONG WHICH WAS THIS ONE AND "JEHOVAH GOD FORMED MAN, AND BREATHED INTO MAN'S NOSTRILS THE BREATH OF LIVES; AND MAN BECAME A LIVING SOUL. (GEN. 2:7)" — *True Christian Religion* 697

The contending swords were there while they speculated and missed the nature of the soul. The true understanding was met with light that lit up the walls. The soul is the essence of the person, the essence of his love and wisdom, perception and understanding. It is not the body, but it looks and feels like the real person. The soul was perfectly manifest. Each person was a soul looking at other souls. Locating it in a gland, brain ventricles or heart was foolish. The soul is the real person.

I'd like to carry this a step beyond Swedenborg's writings by asking whether we can see the soul in this world. Here, I'll put on the cap and gown and answer. Putting on the cap and gown means trying to take on the spirit and quality of the soul itself, silk, opaline (many colors and attributes), soft, wool embroidered with flowers, and a cap (thought) ornamented with roses and sapphires. Picture slowly examining and putting on such a cap and gown. Surely you become closer to the true thought of the soul. It is a world of correspondences. One can feel the spiritual.

I say yes, we can see the soul. We do not see it if we regard the person as just a body. We do see it if we lovingly regard the other person in his central tendencies and qualities. This means looking beyond momentary stress or illness towards the kind of life this person is. It represents a great deal of understanding to see a friend in this light. The most central characteristic of my wife is a love of functional beauty in her surroundings. Out of this one can easily understand she keeps a well-decorated home. She majored in art. She collects paintings, loves music and opera. She is a potter. She has a fantastic memory for houses and especially how functional their layout is. In social interactions she is always trying to bring harmony and avoid discord. Etc. Etc. She finds pretty things wherever she goes. Many features are thereby understood including the host of things in which she has little interest. She is not interested in religion unless there is a religion whose central focus is beauty. That church would find her in the front row.

My own central tendencies are those of a scholar and writer. I need to bring order and clarity to what otherwise is murky. Guess who rewrites the directions for complex equipment and puts labels on storage boxes. I can have a headache and feel ill and dig into Swedenborg and all illness disappears. I have the problem of wanting to read more books than is possible. A high experience for me is to finally have a complete understanding of something and be able to share this with others.

The soul is the unique combination of loves and qualities which make a person what they are. It is relatively manifest and obvious because it shows in his loves, his reactions and even in the nuances of movement and voice quality. This life of a person has central tendencies showing all the time, because it is eternal.

It is useful to look both for our own central tendencies and those of others. Either way, it promotes understanding I am "at home" in scholarship, just as my wife is at home when shaping a pot on the wheel or sketching the layout of a home. Knowing yourself cuts through all the distractions of life and focuses what is most meaningful for the person.

What happened in Swedenborg's search for the soul? He found it in ways far more manifest than the earlier Swedenborg, the philosopher, would have thought possible. It is the whole of the human side to his theology.

But there is a big question we've not asked or answered yet. Why did Swedenborg devote over 10 years of his life to the search for the soul? I implied the answer when I said that, in view of his central tendencies, he was on target in his search for the soul. Now we are dealing with Swedenborg's central tendencies. He was on target because he tended toward the concrete, the real, the human, the useful. If you take his occupation as a geologist and mining engineer as a symbolic correspondent, you will see what I mean. Here was a man who was interested in practical, concrete realities. How best to extract copper? He drifted from an abstract and not useful conception of soul to a detailed understanding of real human experience. His theology is very applicable in life, far more than has yet been shown. Out of the chaotic ground of human experience he sought useful ore. That ore is the understanding brought by seeing people in terms of their central tendencies.

But this is only half the answer to why he worked so hard to find the soul. The soul is given by God, the temple from which God manifests in the person. Above all else Swedenborg was looking for God. He sought the design with which we are cast into existence in hopes of glimpsing the Designer. And he accomplished this quite beyond his fondest hopes. And we too can stand in the field of our central tendencies and looking from them can glimpse something of how we fit into the scheme of things. Though we are a life, we in no respect designed, sustain or even really understand life.

> AND THE LORD FOR THE SAKE OF HIS RECEPTION BY MAN, MAKES IT APPEAR THAT LIFE IS, AS IT WERE, MAN'S.
>
> — *Divine Love and Wisdom* 394

The soul is the borderland from which one can see the Designer. That is what he was really looking for. His looking through persons to God gave his theology an unusually rich human quality, and God was found as the Very Human.

Uses: A Way of Personal and Spiritual Growth

The simplest and most powerful method for personal spiritual development in Swedenborg's theology lies in the idea of uses. Part of its beauty is its simplicity, which permits carrying it out in the midst of ordinary duties and labor, indeed, in any human act. It can be applied anywhere, anytime, by anyone. Part of its power lies in its wonderful concreteness. Much of religion has to do with masses of words and ideas. Use lies in concrete acts. Words are unnecessary. The very concrete immediacy of uses takes us out of ourselves, out into circumstances, out toward others and a larger world.

The range and power of this method have been largely overlooked by students of Swedenborg's writings. Use is often seen as simply a synonym for charity and good works. It is a much more pervasive idea than that, for, as we shall see, it applies to all human acts done in a certain spirit. The method simply cannot be grasped by reading and speculation alone. It must be practiced to see its power. There is no other way! Literally, only in the practice of use may its real potentialities be found. In uses one is attempting to do whatever is at hand very well as a way of reaching out and learning. It is a way of practicing devotion in any work or activity. What hasn't been noticed is a subtle, fast and consistent Divine response in one's inner awareness. This

Divine leading and guidance takes several forms. The complex dynamics of these leadings perfect how one works, correct personal habits and faults, and then lead into general perceptions of the nature of reality. Should you get into this process, you will see that it is powerful and comprehensive enough that no other method of spiritual development is ever needed. The interior response is in terms of what you need to learn here and now. One could not ask for a more personal or pertinent response. And the range of this method not only continuously perfects what you do, but it leads through personal insights and wisdom to experience the Divine. This is the power of the method that has not been particularly well understood or applied. But first, let us look at what Swedenborg really meant by uses. If only one idea could be saved from his writings, this is the one I would choose, for it turns out to be the hinge pin of both personal development and of his whole theology.

Swedenborg's "use" means essentially spiritual function. Suppose we wanted to really grasp the uses of a carpenter. It would not be enough to talk of measuring, sawing and nailing wood together. This is too abstract. We should go to a project under way and walk around in the skeleton of a building under construction. Yet this would not be as good as eventually moving into the house to get the full feeling and impact of the use the carpenter has created. We have breakfast daily in the dining alcove he created and enjoy the view of the garden. It is this possibility of living in and enjoying the space he created that is a concrete knowing of his use. Use has this immensely concrete aspect, in this case a house, but it also has a personal or spiritual aspect, the qualities of living in it. In uses Swedenborg is viewing the whole of creation in both this concrete and interior spiritual aspect. In this larger way *we are a design or use* walking around in and enjoying a design use called creation. As we will see, use is a profoundly human way of appreciating existence. Taken separately from its human uses, a house is a strange tangle of wood and materials having no real rhyme, reason or purpose. But the dining alcove, for instance, makes good sense seen from its human functioning. It is just off the kitchen, handy to the preparing of food. One can be sheltered while eating and yet look out on the garden which softens the light of day. The details of the form of the house make their best sense from the viewpoint of human use. This human being, lived-in quality, is the ultimate spiritual nature of use.

TRUTH IS . . . LIKE A GARMENT; WHEN NOT BEING WORN, IT IS MERELY PIECES OF MATERIAL ADAPTED FOR A BODY, BUT WHEN IT IS PUT ON, IT BECOMES CLOTHING WITH A HUMAN BEING INSIDE IT.

— *Divine Love and Divine Wisdom* 150

Just as the use a family would make of the house created by the carpenter governed his work, the uses of creation is the end which governs its form. The end or purpose governs all the details of the design and hence of the form. Hence spiritual function or use is the key to the design of creation. It is a way of looking at creation that gathers all the tiny details together and enables one to see through time to the way the whole operates. This is the spiritual or overall design.

THE UNIVERSAL LAW IN REGARD TO CORRESPONDENCE IS THAT THE SPIRITUAL THING CONDITIONS ITSELF FOR THE USE THAT IS ITS END-IN-VIEW, . . . AND CLOTHES IT WITH INTERMEDIARY THINGS PROVIDED FOR THAT PURPOSE, SO THAT FINALLY A FORM IS CREATED SERVING THE END-IN-VIEW. IN THAT FORM, WHAT IS SPIRITUAL OCCUPIES THE POSITION OF "END," THE USE THE POSITION OF "CAUSE," AND WHAT IS NATURAL THE POSITION OF "EFFECT." IN THE SPIRITUAL WORLD, HOWEVER, WHAT IS SUBSTANTIAL IS IN PLACE OF WHAT IS NATURAL. ALL THINGS IN MAN ARE FORMS OF THIS DESCRIPTION.

— *Divine Love and Divine Wisdom* 73

[EVERYTHING IN HEAVEN, IN THE WORLD, AND IN THE HUMAN BODY] BOTH GREAT AND SMALL, WAS CREATED FROM USE, IN USE, AND FOR USE. A PART IN WHICH THIS LAST, ITS BEING FOR USE, CEASES, IS SEPARATED AS HARMFUL . . .

— *Apocalypse Explained* 1194.2

So, like a tumor, if it interferes with use, it is cut out and killed. Use is a way of considering the design, function and purpose of everything. We cannot see the whole of uses since we cannot see across an eternity of time, but we can clearly see a portion of these uses. And, in this portion, we see enough to sense the overall design. We see through our uses into the useful design of all things. This is appropriate because in our uses we are the image of the whole. The uses the carpenter put into the house are best appreciated by the family living there. In a larger sense we are the family living in the house built for us. By feeling out the qualities of the design, we are entering into the ends of the Builder. Daily, and even moment to moment, in our appreciation of the house given us, the ends of the Builder are spreading out through time. This is both an image of our ordinary experience and of the designing of creation. It is through our involvement in uses that we appreciate the universe as series within series of uses.

This brings to the idea of uses something that at first seems strange. We keep coming back to the image of man, or, in a sexless sense, back to humanness or personhood. Is this simply our limitation that we see things through ourselves? Here Swedenborg gives an answer that, at first, may trouble the understanding. No, it is not simply our limitation. It is the other way around. In the tiniest aspect of our form we are the image of the whole, of all there is. At first it seemed odd to me that Swedenborg kept referring to anatomical functions as theological images. But listen to his description of the human body as an image of the whole design of creation.

> TRUE, A PERSON IS MADE UP OF COUNTLESS DIFFERENT COMPONENTS, BOTH OVERALL AND IN HIS PARTS. OVERALL, HE IS MADE UP OF MEMBERS, ORGANS AND VISCERA, SECONDARILY OF CHAINS OF FIBERS, NERVES, AND BLOOD VESSELS—OF MEMBERS WITHIN MEMBERS, AND THEN OF PARTS WITHIN PARTS. STILL WHEN A PERSON ACTS, HE ACTS AS A UNIT. HEAVEN IS LIKE THIS, UNDER THE LORD'S AUTHORITY AND GUIDANCE. THE REASON SO MANY DIFFERENT THINGS ACT AS A UNIT IS THAT THERE IS NOT A SINGLE THING INVOLVED THAT DOES NOT DO SOMETHING FOR THE LARGER WHOLE

AND FULFILL A FUNCTION. THE WHOLE FULFILLS A FUNCTION FOR ITS PARTS AND THE PARTS FULFILL FUNCTIONS FOR THE WHOLE . . . SO THEY TAKE CARE FOR EACH OTHER, KEEP EACH OTHER IN VIEW, AND ARE ASSEMBLED INTO THE KIND OF FORM IN WHICH EACH AND EVERY ELEMENT REFLECTS THE WHOLE AND ITS "GOOD." THIS IS THE REASON THEY ACT AS A UNIT. —*Heaven and Hell* 63–64

The lungs work with blood, which works with all the tissues; particular uses fitting together that there may be an overall use, that the person may live and act. And the person takes care of his body and its organs. This is also the image of society. The farmers work with packers, who work with grocery stores that we might eat and live. This is also an image of heaven, where individuals make their unique contribution to societies (which are like organs of the body) which contribute to the One Man, the Grand Man. Every time Swedenborg's Grand Man puzzles you, look to your own form, which is an image of all there is. *The reason that all these patterns of uses working together tend toward heaven is that in uses we look across from the part toward the whole*. What use are my hands unless they do something, and in this doing I have reached beyond myself toward creation. The carpenter's uses extend into the family and through them into their friends and contacts. The great wonder of use as a method is that it enables us to go beyond ourselves, to reach through creation. Swedenborg easily sees from a limited use to the larger sphere of uses, creation.

THE MUSCLES AND ORGANS OF SENSE, AS THE SIGHT (FOR INSTANCE), HAVE RESPECT TO A COMMON USE, NAMELY THE INTERNAL SIGHT; WHEREFORE THEY ALSO ARE FOR USE AND FROM USE. INTERNAL SIGHT, OR THOUGHT, HAS RESPECT TO A COMMON END, WHICH IS THE GOOD OF SOCIETY IN GENERAL AND IN UNIVERSAL OVER THE EARTH; WHEREFORE ALL THINGS OF THOUGHT WILL BE USES AND TENDING TO THAT END . . .

— *Spiritual Diary* 3574

God designed the universe as a use and even series within series of uses. Our bodily form is an example of this and, hence, we are an image of the whole. Swedenborg uses man or Grand Man or the Divine Human as the form of all uses.

> GOD AS A MAN IS THE FORM ITSELF OF ALL USES, FROM WHICH FORM ALL USES IN THE CREATED UNIVERSE DERIVE THEIR ORIGIN, THUS THE CREATED UNIVERSE, VIEWED AS TO USES, IS AN IMAGE OF HIM.
>
> —*Divine Love and Wisdom* 298

We see in this not so much how God looks externally, but how creation lives and functions internally. In a similar way we do not "see" the carpenter's real uses as boards nailed together but in the lived-in qualities of the space and shelter created. We do not think of ourselves as bones and tissues arranged thus, but as one life which lives in thus and so ways. The image of the Grand Man is not really bones and tissues but all life seen as a one of which we and the whole of creation is a representative image. If we were wise and reflective elephants, would it be appropriate to see the design of the whole as the Grand Elephant? Indeed yes, for it would only be through our living quality as elephants that we could sense the quality of the whole! The image of the Grand Man does not elevate man so much as it is a way to see into the whole through our functioning or uses. You wonder how angels grasp a truth? Hold something tightly in your hand until you can see through your life. If my image puzzles you, hold tighter and longer. This is called seeing through the life, which is essentially what the idea of uses is. Through uses we reach outside of ourselves and see through our life into all life. Use is the fitting together of things, how each fits with and contributes to others. It is a way of looking at things that gets beyond the thing-in-itself to see how it fits into the whole.

> THAT THE DIVINE LOVE WHICH IS LIFE ITSELF AND WHICH IS THE LORD, IS IN THE FORM OF THE FORMS OF ALL USES, WHICH FORM IS MAN, CAN BE NOWHERE BETTER SEEN THAN IN THE CREATION OF THE UNIVERSE AND THEN OF THE EARTH AND OF ALL THINGS IN

THEM BOTH. FOR, BY CREATION THERE IS NOTHING ON THE EARTH THAT IS NOT MADE FOR USE. THE WHOLE MINERAL KINGDOM IS FULL OF USES; THERE IS NOT A PARTICLE OF DUST IN IT, NOR ANY PIECE OF SOIL FORMED OF SUCH PARTICLES, THAT IS NOT OF USE. THE WHOLE VEGETABLE KINGDOM IS FULL OF USES . . . THE WHOLE ANIMAL KINGDOM, ALSO, IS FULL OF USES; THERE IS NOT AN ANIMAL, FROM THE LITTLE WORM TO THE LION, THAT IS NOT OF USE, AND THAT IS NOT ALSO THE FORM OF ITS USE. . . . IN A WORD, EVERY POINT IN THE CREATED UNIVERSE AND IN CREATED BEINGS IS A USE; IN FACT, IT IS A SUCCESSIVELY EXPANDING SERIES OF USES FROM THE USE IN FIRST THINGS TO THE USE IN ULTIMATES, THUS FROM ONE USE TO ANOTHER IN UNBROKEN SUCCESSION—CLEAR PROOF THAT THE CREATOR AND FORMER, WHO IS THE LORD, IS THE INFINITE ENFOLDING OF ALL USES, IN HIS ESSENCE LOVE, AND IN HIS FORM MAN IN WHOM THAT ENFOLDING IS.

—*Divine Love and Divine Wisdom* [Post.] 20

How does this operate through a person? The whole spiritual world operates through the love and affections. The love of the life is the inmost tendency of the individual. It is when the deepest tendency and love is expressed in act that the individual comes into his highest use.

. . . IF LOVE DOES NOT BECOME DEED IT CEASES TO BE LOVE, THE DEED BEING THE EFFECTING OF ITS PURPOSE, AND THAT IN WHICH IT HAS ITS EXISTENCE. —*Divine Love and Divine Wisdom* [Post.] 38

There are several implications of this. Loves or affections need to do something to realize themselves. Swedenborg makes a direct equivalence between uses and charity. A person who is useless is thereby uncharitable. Charity is to do something of uses beyond one's limited self. One feels most free when giving his love realization as act. Then one's highest use will be along the lines of one's deepest love of the life. This formula allows considerable range for individual differences. One may find his highest use when building things, another when singing and entertaining others, another in caring for children, etc. Throughout, the idea of use is *reality*. Love or charity becomes real in use. Performing uses really is to do something. Something gets done.

There is a tendency to think of uses in a limited sense as charity, in which one does good for the neighbor. Swedenborg defines it in such a broad way as to include all a person's acts. Uses can be for one's self:

> THE USES FOR SUSTAINING THE BODY COMPRISE ITS NOURISHMENT, CLOTHING, HABITATION, RECREATION AND ENJOYMENT, PROTECTION AND CONSERVATION OF STATE.
>
> —*Divine Love and Wisdom* 331

It includes providing for one's self and loved ones:

> GOOD USES ARE PROVIDING ONESELF AND ONE'S OWN WITH THE NECESSARIES OF LIFE . . . —*Heaven and Hell* 361

> WHAT IS MEANT [BY USE] IS CARRYING OUT ONE'S DUTY, WHETHER IN THE PUBLIC SERVICE, OR IN BUSINESS, OR IN EMPLOYMENT, RIGHTLY, FAITHFULLY, HONESTLY AND JUSTLY; WHEN THIS IS BEING DONE, THEN THE WELFARE OF THE GENERAL BODY OF PEOPLE OR MANKIND IS BEING CARED FOR . . .
>
> —*Divine Love and Divine Wisdom* 133

Neither wealth nor business is excluded.

> RICHES ARE TO BE ESTEEMED FOR THE USE TO WHICH THEY ARE PUT; LIKEWISE THE SCIENCES, PHILOSOPHY, THE GIFTS OF GENIUS.
>
> —*Spiritual Diary* 112

> BUSINESS IS SUCH A GOOD WHEN IT IS THE END-LOVE AND MONEY IS A MEDIATE, SUBSERVIENT LOVE, AS IT IS ONLY WHEN THE BUSINESSMAN SHUNS AND IS AVERSE TO FRAUD AND BAD PRACTICES AS SIN. —*Divine Providence* 220.11

Since we all pretty much have some work or duties, are we not all then in the uses? Not necessarily. Swedenborg is making a subtle distinction that has to do with our purposes. We have two shoe repairmen, both making a living at this trade. One has as his aim making the most money. He cuts corners on materials and workmanship. He has to grind out as many repairs as possible. The second also is concerned with profit, but he enjoys meeting customers, talking of shoe problems, and he enjoys his craft. The aim of the first is *his* profit above the customer's welfare. The aim of the second is profit through the customer's welfare. This is the difference between hell and heaven. If you visited these two shops, you probably would quickly sense the difference. If we sent in a shoe repair expert, he could probably find the difference in the repaired shoes. The idea of uses is intimately related to quality. Could not the second man be even more charitable by cutting prices and thereby giving away his services as a charity? No. This would overlook his obligations to himself and his family. He has a difficult judgment to make in relation to his needs and the needs of others. His needs have to be met as well as those of his customers. If he gives away his services and materials, he will soon be out of business and no longer of service, while having harmed himself and his family. The charity is to be toward the self, loved ones and others.

The use that leads to heaven includes self, loved ones and others, and indeed creation itself. The use that leads to hell puts one's self supreme. There is so much deception practiced that it may take some while to figure out which is which, but the internal end is diametrically opposite. Two men own and operate a clothing store. Outwardly they do the same thing, sell men's clothes. Look closer. One quickly sizes up the customer's wants. He likes this color, that style. Let's see—perhaps this is what he wants? Everyone is different and he enjoys finding and serving these differences. He is pleased to see the clothes he sold appearing here and there around town. The other clothing salesman pushes this or that, touts it as a bargain. The profit-making sale is his end, not the customer's needs. He serves only himself. The first salesman serves himself and the other person. It is a mutual benefit. It may take a fairly close study and feeling out of the human situation even to see this difference, especially as the second man learns artfully to conceal his ends.

Swedenborg's description of heaven and hell is not a remote spiritual judgment. Look closely. It is built right into any act. The first clothing salesman, in being curious of, and sensitive to the needs of customers, is already opening out beyond himself to the larger community. It is as simple as that. The second man, by attempting to overcome the resistance of the customer, to get his own ends, has already started a closing in, a limiting of himself which is the implication of hell. The outcome is built into the subtlety of their acts. Uses are heavenwards. That is, they involve a reaching out, an expansion. The opposite act is for one's self above everything else. It constricts into the self. It closes off and limits. In the work situation it also makes one in conflict with the environment. Work simply has to be gotten through so you can do what you want. Work is in your way. In uses one reaches through the task at hand beyond one's self. Uses involves an attitude that is sensitive to the environment. The useful person sees what needs doing and does it. But one can also be useful in ordinary social conversation by trying to sense the other person and his needs and responding to these. But then how can one reach out towards one's own needs? By taking care of yourself with rest, proper diet, exercise, recreation, etc., so that you might remain a useful instrument. Healthful living is being useful toward yourself. Unhealthy living can not only make you useless but can even make you a negative value that has to be supported by others. But carry it a step further beyond simply living by the rules of health. Your greatest uses rest upon being very sensitive and considerate to yourself so that you might find and eventually carry out your unique and highest uses. Like the clothing salesman, who has to make a difficult judgment between his need for profit and the customer's needs, to find your greatest use also requires judgment. The pressure of the environment is to do this and that. One can easily become swallowed up in these pressures and never discover one's own gifts. This slow and sensitive discovery may involve saying no to pressures; no, I want some time to explore this or that because it interests me. There are plenty of mysteries in applying uses to one's self. Sometimes I feel depressed, out of sorts and interested in nothing. I assume my instrument for uses, myself, has been neglected. I try to approach myself with great consideration, searching out what I need. Let's see. I'd feel better just to take a shower and then walk in the garden for awhile. I treat myself like a stranger who is ill and needs some kind of care. I do this for a time until interest returns and I can return again to uses. Usefulness toward ourself is as mysterious, reaching out, and searching a process as the development of our highest use. In it I treat myself as a great unknown to reach out and discover. Again, the attitude is one of reaching out, searching. In my work as a psychotherapist I've known many Christians who neglected themselves to the point of producing madness. They thought charity was only for others—never for self. It is as difficult to discover what is ultimately the highest charity towards one's self as it is for the most puzzling stranger.

In any act, whether brushing your hair, fixing a gadget, or taking care of a customer, the basic attitude of uses is a respectful search. Devotion would be a better word here. *Uses, as a spiritual method, is an attempt to search through the task at hand. It means being very faithful to the task at hand.* Working wood, it means to respect the grain of the wood. Speaking to a person, it means really trying to sense him. Washing my hands, it means cleaning them patiently and well. This faithful, devotional attitude in uses means first and foremost that one will learn and perfect the task at hand. The medieval stonemason who built the cathedrals is an image of the mastery such an attitude leads to. These masons became familiar with the qualities of stone and through that were able to express their highest ideals. Uses, devotion to the task at hand, leads necessarily to skill and quality in workmanship. It is the opposite of simply getting tasks out of the way. Uses in a way of speaking to all there is. It is spiritual communication. You wish to speak to God? Do the task at hand with the greatest faithfulness and devotion. I must emphasize, any task. The idea that only under certain circumstances, in acts of charity, can you practice uses, is wrong. Any act. I am practicing what is possibly my highest use now by writing. This is the task that has come to hand to be practiced with devotion. My wife calls me to dinner. How about a cheery word and a compliment on what she has prepared. And how can I practice uses while eating? By appreciating the food and being sensitive to my bodily needs—enough to eat but not too much, as though I am taking care of a stranger. Any act.

I've often reflected that a spiritual method should be open to all. Suppose a person is sick in bed and can't do anything? How could he be useful? He can attempt to be little trouble to others and be as cheerful and comforting as possible to those who visit. Uses. Few of us will be statesmen or stateswomen who serve great uses in society. But all of us can attempt to serve uses within our station and occupation. You live alone in the woods? There are lots of plants and animals you can help. It might be enough just to be considerate of the plants and animals that live there too. Who cannot serve some use, whatever his place? You are stuck in the world's dullest job, screwing nuts on bolts in a factory. How to be of use? Perform your job well. Reflect on the use to others of the machine you are working on. Be of good cheer to fellow workers. Well, how can you be useful when not working? It is Sunday morning and you are reading the Sunday paper with the family. You can still attempt use. Be of good cheer to other family members. Consider the children want the funny papers first. In reading the news, reflect on the situation of other people in remote parts of the world. There is no situation in which you are really prevented from reaching beyond yourself, which is to be of use. Locked in a prison Solzhenitsyn was memorizing names and situations so that he might one day prepare books of widespread use. Even if he never got to write or even live outside of prison, he was trying to live beyond himself and, hence, spiritually lived in a wider sphere than the man simply caught in the gloom of prison life. Uses is an attempt to live beyond the self even if it is just one inch beyond the finger tips.

Use also involves pleasure.

> IT IS, HOWEVER, GRANTED TO INTERRUPT LABORS BY VARIOUS THINGS THAT ARE DONE IN THE COMPANY OF OTHERS; THESE THINGS ARE RECREATIONS, AND THUS THEY ARE USES ALSO.
>
> — *Apocalypse Explained* 1194.2

> . . . A PERSON'S DELIGHTS ARE OF THE SAME QUALITY AS HIS USES, AND ON THE SAME LEVEL AS HIS AFFECTION FOR USE.
>
> —*Heaven and Hell* 402

The Puritan view is that whatever leads to heaven should involve suffering and not pleasure. But it is characteristic that people serving their greatest use will also be enjoying themselves. Part of this pleasure comes because your use is your means of extending your powers outside yourself. The good shoe repairman enjoys sharing his knowledge of what is needed with the customer bothered by a pair of shoes. At the same time he gets a job and a profit. The gardener enjoys watering the dry, limp plant that needs it. Why? Because by this simple act the plant comes back to life and brightens his life.

> . . . EVERYTHING THAT LOVE DOES IT CALLS USE.
>
> —*Divine Love and Wisdom* 336

The link between feeling and uses has been implied in all the examples given. We come into our uses when we combine what we enjoy doing with what needs doing. This very much implies a marriage between the unique tendencies in the individual and the needs of the environment. For the individual it means giving expression and reality to one's inner tendencies. It also means individual differences. A few people are gathered chatting in the patio. One tends to a distressed kitten caught in a tree. Another manages to take care of plants while talking. A third becomes very involved with what the other person is trying to express. All uses, but varied.

The idea of uses rests on some subtle distinctions, but once you become involved in these spiritual matters, they become more and more obvious. The idea of uses involves any attempt to reach or even just see and understand beyond yourself. The outcome is fairly predictable. You will live in a wider sphere than those focused only on themselves. The clothing salesman who enjoys seeing his products worn here and there about town has a wider sphere of life than the salesman oriented only to his own profit. The one who attempts this reach beyond the self is thereby rewarded. The reward is so automatic that you will not be surprised. If my end is myself foremost, I am constricting my sphere to me. If my end is to learn, or to do something useful, I live out into a larger sphere. The results or "judgment" is forecast in the quality of the act.

The realization of one's real ends is part of the inner subtlety in uses. But there is a larger one which I have called the Divine response. Some would debate this; they prefer to remove the Divine as far as possible from human acts. I call it a Divine response because it is exceedingly wise, with a long range view as to our needs and ultimate uses. We attempt to do something in uses. The response comes in moments, flows in and opens our interior sight. It is so subtle and interior that it could easily be overlooked. Though I can give examples, you will have to try it yourself to confirm this is a universal process. I am driving a car on errands around town. I keep getting caught behind slow people. While waiting for a car to make a turn, I think I'll practice uses now. It occurs to me there are so many slow cars today because I am impatient. If I could drive more patiently, we would all be safer. I'll try, but it is difficult. The sequence, I will practice uses, I see my fault, is a common one. I had not intended to confront my fault, I had only intended to perform this use of driving well, but it led to seeing my fault. Years later I can remember exactly where I was stopped in the car when this insight was given to me. The moment had become memorable. I saw that everyone else's slowness was simply my impatience.

An example. I am a writer. I am trying to understand how to say this to be of the most use to you. Reflecting on this, I put down my pencil, pick up and fondle an eraser. It is an unusually effective type of eraser I go out of my way to buy. It then occurs to me, if enough people see its superior qualities, it will survive. But, of course, what is of the greatest use tends to last. The great classic works, including Swedenborg's, survived because many found them useful. I see this as a general principle. I had asked how to make this most useful. I was not answered how I could do so. The Divine response was, in effect, to say what is useful lasts. Keep your eye on uses if you want your work to survive. The sequence, I make a petition (how to make this useful), forgetting, doing something by chance (handling the eraser), and suddenly seeing a general principle, is common. The answer given did not serve my ends (how can I . . . ?), but rather was a wiser answer about the general nature of reality. If I keep trying for uses, I will be working toward what lasts the longest, for uses are the design of eternity. It looks like a small thing. I make an effort, and I am given an answer in an unexpected direction. The wisdom of the answer is a very gentle turning. It says, "Don't worry about how *you* will do. By keeping your eye on uses, you open toward what will last, the eternal." Still fondling the eraser, I question the wonder of the eternal which I now sense. The answer comes, "It is the real." And now the reality of the things about me hit me. This is an example of seeing into general principles when practicing uses.

A more common type of Divine response appears in any manual labor. I am washing dishes attempting to be of use. I notice dirt on the dish I was about to put to dry. The response is, "Here, do this job better." I go on attempting to be of use and get the dishes clean, and I sense that I am too impatient. If I rush the dishes, I'll finish one or two minutes faster, to what end? The response was, in effect, "You are too impatient." The Divine response in manual labor is often to be shown how to do the work better or to learn of one's own personal faults. This is so common a response that I'd be very surprised at anyone who attempts uses in manual labor who does not have a similar outcome.

You might object, "Why call this the Divine response?" I would not debate the matter. But I would say at the time I am only aware of attempting to reach beyond myself. How to improve the job is a discovery. But even more, I had not intended to illustrate my own faults! You have to work some while with uses to get used to both the intimacy and the clever immediacy of the Divine response. You also get used to the idea that, much of the time, you will be shown something of your own nature. You learn not only how to do things well, but you simultaneously learn of yourself. Ultimately, these two become as one. The one who understands himself does things well indeed. But again, I remind you that you cannot simply speculate on these things. Try uses in manual labor for months or years and then tell us what you discovered. I don't know how to say this emphatically enough. The doctrine of uses is not a thing to learn and speculate on.

It can only be really understood in useful acts. And to see the Divine's response in these acts, I am speaking of a long and careful examination.

This idea of using acts as a means of talking directly with God is an ancient one that has appeared in all cultures. I am reminded of the Zen monk whose job it was to clean toilets in a monastery. The whole purpose of life in the monastery was the enlightenment that is a seeing into God and All There Is. How does this jibe with cleaning toilets? Fortunately, he used his menial task as The Way at hand for him. At first in the cleaning he was taught much of cleaning so that he probably produced some of the cleanest toilets of all time. He was also shown much of his own nature and faults. Then he began seeing general principles in his work. Finally, after all this step-by-step preparation, he found the One, the design of all creation. God came forth and cleaned through his hands. His wisdom became apparent and he was elected abbot of the monastery. But he loved The Way that had opened for him, so he continued to clean the toilets. Examples from every culture and time of this process could be multiplied. But Swedenborg is one of the few who have elevated this simple process many have discovered into the theological principle by which everything is designed.

As you get into the practice of uses, there are a number of subtle aspects and discoveries. Precisely how does one practice uses, since it can be in any human act? By attempting to go outside and beyond yourself. Fixing machinery? By giving the whole attention to the functional qualities of the machine. Talking with a friend? By giving one's whole attention to the qualities and needs of the friend. But the quality of your end comes into play. Your end may be simply to fix the machine, and that is all you may get. Your end could also be to learn of yourself as a craftsman and then that will occur, too. You might concentrate on being of use to other through repair. Or you might try to see into heaven while fixing the engine.

You will soon discover that it is not really a self-directed conscious process that is involved. You wonder of heaven for a few moments but soon get caught up in the operation of this thingamajig. One of the discoveries is that you direct yourself for very little time and, more often, you are caught up in what is at hand. This is not bad. Your seeking heaven was your brief petition. The "random" thoughts, feelings, and bits of learning are the Divine response. In effect, you need to get caught up in the task at hand in order to get proprium or ego out of the way. The discoveries and lessons sneak in when you are out of the way. The process occurs spontaneously on the edge of consciousness, like influx. Yet it occurs so fast, in a half light of awareness, that it is also helpful to reflect afterwards on what you learn, to fix it in memory. This process of petitioning, getting caught up in the task, being shown subtle lessons, and then trying to recall and fix them is typical of both spiritual and psychological discovery. You cannot continuously hold in mind being useful, like a loud, never-ending cry, without drowning out the spontaneous response one is to get. So forgetting yourself and getting caught up in the task is a profound part of The Way. Typically, you are really into the task and enjoying yourself when the insights are given. Then time passes as in a moment and fatigue is little known. This is one sign loves are being realized in use, for you are fully involved and enjoying yourself with little sense of time or fatigue. You can get some glimpse of the love of your life by reviewing circumstances in which this has tended to occur to you. Writing must be near the love of my life, for with the right assignment I have researched and written nine hours a day, only to be surprised later that I forgot to eat. When I finally sat down for supper the writing was still bubbling over in my head, amending and adding to what had already been written.

I said in the beginning that, seen at its highest, uses is a way to the experience of heaven. This is no exaggeration. The key is in knowing what you are looking for and in appreciating what is given. If you think of heaven as specific streets, people, etc., you won't see it. If you think of heaven just as Swedenborg has defined uses, then it is much easier to see. Heaven begins to be seen in a relaxed attitude in which things are seen fitting together. I see it in the garden. All these flowers and plants living together around my patio, watered by my wife. I appreciate she cares for them and they give back the beauty of their presence. It is a circle of mutual caring and support, caring for my wife, who cares for the garden, that cares for me. But you will say this is just a representation. Heaven is elsewhere. Is heaven really outside the circle of this mutual caring? Not really. Besides, it is by savoring these little views of heaven that larger experiences become possible. The one who says heaven can only be experienced after you die has removed it and made it difficult to experience its qualities. By savoring and learning from little glimpses, seeing more becomes possible. One that is frequently given me is a visual representation of the design of all creation. I see an intensely alive center that I cannot really look at. Out of it radiate in all directions multicolored lines which go forth with easy grace and then curve back in and fall toward their source. This is an image of the endless Life of The One cast into existence with easy grace and returning from its created forms into its own being. Or, on occasion, when caught up in the pleasure of uses I suddenly sense the unity of all uses, as though the universe was a single Aliveness. I am saying that a good part of seeing and understanding inner visions rests in part on simply looking for them and in savoring and appreciating what is given. The more you experience this sort of thing, the plainer heaven becomes, and the more Swedenborg's theology opens up. If you constantly look how you can fit in and contribute to your situation, the issues of your own greatness recede. You'll then be given gentle images which gradually intensify and become the thing itself you sought. Another way of saying it is, appreciate every glimpse given and more will be given.

Above my desk is a large black and white print of the medieval city of Dusseldorf. In the foreground I see the Rhenus Fluvius, Rhine River, with many people in a barge, several anchored sailing vessels and some people rowing. On the other bank of the river there is a large medieval city with many public buildings and churches with tall spires. I see the efforts of many to produce the best they know of. Heaven is like this, each contributing what he can to the whole. There is also a kind of relief from selfhood. I need not hold up myself contra others. Rather, each contributes what he can and is honored to be able to enjoy the great city of the whole. Uses overcomes the painful nuisance of big selfness. It is a way of fitting in, contributing what you can to the whole, that you might live in and enjoy the larger whole that is created. The citizen of Dusseldorf out rowing the boat isn't much in himself. He didn't build all the tall spires. Yet he contributes what he can and can enjoy the whole that is created. He lives in the sphere of uses that open out from his finger tips. We are each that citizen of Dusseldorf out rowing our little boat and able to look at and enjoy the whole we have contributed toward.

I have emphasized that the spiritual practice of uses in any act is a way of reaching out. Any person, any act, any time. Your attitude or end you have in mind is fairly critical. The Divine response is not always what you seek. It is in terms of what is most useful to you. Let's say you practice uses in gardening. You seek a vision of God. But you keep getting back simple lessons about gardening. The Divine response says, in effect, you are a dumb gardener with much to learn. Don't be put off by this. This is the finest lesson you can get now. That is what you need and deserve. Savor it. Learn to be a good gardener. Then one day, when you are looking for more boneheaded lessons of gardening, you may find insight into your personal traits being given to you. Having learned step one, step two has begun. Now you are learning about gardening and yourself. Later, even this changes and you are given insights into the general nature of reality. Long after it was first sought, visions of heaven might be given. Why this sequence? My guess is that the larger view of heaven could not appropriately be given at first because your experience was not grounded. If given immediately, it would not have the reality it would have after grounding in the concrete. Similarly, I am quite convinced that Swedenborg had to go through much discoveries of affect and feeling in his *Journal of Dreams* period before he could really grasp theology. Otherwise, he would have had a theology without love and feeling, which is less than half a theology. I believe the lessons given in the spiritual practices of uses are the most useful ones to the individual at that time. The opposite sequence, one seeking the concrete and being given spiritual lessons, also occurs in those well developed spiritually. As long as you are seeking, you need not be too concerned whether you are being given the right level of answers. That is decided from a higher wisdom.

Is it essential that one know and seek God? Here my answer will be a little surprising. There will be those who seek through uses that don't even believe in God. My guess is that knowing higher visions is possible and seeking them will speed up the recognition of them. But, on the other side of the coin, I believe so much in the wisdom within the process that I suspect those who really look into uses will discover God or their equivalent of Him in spite of nonbelief. I am saying that the internals of the process are universal and are the same for all regardless of belief. At best, belief that something could occur may only speed up recognition of its occurring. In the internals of this process we discover a "God" that is somewhat different and far more real than the usual Christian concept of God. Those who look outward in uses begin to experience the interconnectedness and interdependence of all things. They already are living in and moving in what Swedenborg means by heaven and God. But the concrete, ever present, matter of factness and practically of their experience may make it difficult for those caught in religious abstractions to recognize the substance of these experiences. This is an awesome idea, but it reinforces the reality of what Swedenborg is talking about. Those who enjoy uses already participate in and experience the interconnectedness of all things, which is here called heaven. Those outside the experience of uses may debate meanings. The one who experiences it may not even be able to answer the debate intelligently. But who is actually closer to heaven, the one who enjoys being useful or the one, who can cleverly debate the meaning of heaven? The scriptural answer is quite clear. Love in act, being useful, charity is supreme. Better a moment's consideration of another person, or of anything, than all the debates. Rather than the right religious terms (whether Christian, Buddhist, or whatever), it is better to enter on spiritual experiences which open out from trying to be useful. So, I am saying, even the right words and religious ideas are not essential. The right concept is to try to be useful. If you consistently try to be useful and look closely at what occurs in the process, you will discover heaven and the One. The most my description of the process does is speed up your recognition of what occurs. But the religious ideas that lie outside of your own practice and experience are just useless sounds, soon forgotten. *You can only understand and appreciate the aspects of use actually made real, experienced and realized in your life.*

Use is the concrete foundation of Swedenborg's theology. The natural world can't be this foundation; it is just things. Use is a spiritual thing, and from this it is a basic element of theology. There is, for me, a kind of wonderful mystery in the very spiritual thingness of uses.

USES ARE THE EFFECTS IN WHICH THE END HAS EXISTENCE.
—*Divine Love and Divine Wisdom* 129

TRUTHS WHICH ARE COMMITTED TO LIFE [OR ACTS] BECOME USES.
—*Arcana Coelestia* 5527

CHARITY, VIEWED IN ITSELF, DOES NOT BECOME CHARITY UNTIL IT COMES INTO ACT AND BECOMES A WORK.
—*Arcana Coelestia* 6073

JUST AS AFFECTION IS THE ESSENTIAL MAN, AND USE IS ITS EFFECT AND OPERATION, AND THE FIELD OR TRAINING-GROUND AS IT WERE FOR ITS EXERCISE, AND JUST AS THERE CAN BE NO AFFECTION UNLESS IT HAS A "SUBJECT," SO TOO, A MAN'S LIFE'S AFFECTION CANNOT EXIST WITHOUT HAVING ITS USE; AND BECAUSE THE AFFECTION AND THE USE MAKE A ONE, SO THE QUALITY OF A MAN WHO IS AN AFFECTION, IS RECOGNIZED FROM HIS USE; ONLY WITH DIFFICULTY AND IMPERFECTLY IN THE NATURAL WORLD, BUT IN THE SPIRITUAL WORLD CLEARLY AND FULLY . . .

THE REASON THE ETERNAL LIFE THAT EACH ONE HAS, IS IN ACCORDANCE WITH HIS AFFECTION FOR USE, IS THAT THIS IS THE ESSENTIAL MAN, AND CONSEQUENTLY SUCH AS THE AFFECTION IS, SUCH IS HE. —*Divine Love and Divine Wisdom* 48

The endless richness of uses becomes apparent when you do the same routine task in a devoted way. You then discover a never ending series of learnings in the same task. Among many other discoveries is that the basis of personal identity changes. Early in the practice of uses it seems that one is simply trying to do the task at hand better. You are trying. Later in the series of learnings it is as though the task is being done through you. You are closer to an observer watching something being done. It goes well by itself. You begin to feel yourself to be what Swedenborg calls a recipient vessel. At first you *try* to do good. Later good is simply done through you. Much later the experience is of God acting through you and you find yourself involved in acts which transcend your normal capacities. Then there is but One acting through all, and you feel like an awed spectator watching processes quite beyond your limits. The process of lessening personal identity and an increase of Divine awareness is a usual spiritual development. But not knowing this, some become frightened and disturbed when it occurs.

What are we really doing when practicing uses? First, we are looking beyond ourselves. I am baking bread and considering how it is done to make a perfect product. Or I am considering my family who will eat it. Or I am considering the symbolic meaning of bread. These levels of looking beyond the self can be arranged in a complex hierarchy all the way to reflecting on how my hands work to looking for the Divine in the process. In a very long repetitive process, it is easier to examine the various levels and eventually look at the whole hierarchy. We have in effect a process within a process. Outwardly I am making bread, but this process is used as an anchor and focus for an inward process which is far more extensive and complex. The outer focus helps keep it on track, for certain things must be done to make good bread. Regardless of any inner process, there is an actual product to provide good smells and taste when taken out of the oven. The inner process is more of a devotion and a wondering and searching. It has a center focused on baking bread and a productive inner fringe of experiences. I am reflecting on how my hands work, I forget myself, suddenly I am amazed at the complexity of my movements, a complexity not really directed by me. I used to be amazed at my forgetting my focus of attention in the process, but I later found the forgetting is part of the subtle creative inner experience coming in. After the forgetting, you may suddenly have an insight or a memory or a thought of something needing doing, apparently unrelated to the process at hand. It has a relationship, it was represented here in your acts; but you would have to stop everything and reexamine to find the connection. What role does the initial seeking uses play? Much of this process can occur in any labor even without seeking uses. But it is also more likely to be overlooked and become useless. The initial seeking makes it more likely you will notice and remember when something useful is given to you. With practice, the process becomes more of a single creative whole unfolding continuously while working. Then you may see the reverse of the above process. In the above it looks as though you set it going by seeking uses and then something is given you. With practice, you will also see the reverse of this. Something is always being given you and your impulse to seek is also given to you, out of the blue, so you are reminded to seek what you will soon find.

If this makes you begin to think that uses is inwardly a very rich, complex and subtle process, then you begin to see it well. The "normal" worker is just trying to do a task and busily discarding the inner hints, leads and insights given. The seeker of uses is perfecting the task and all its inward components. In the initial stages, when you still think you initiate the process, you may have an essentially foolish direction. For instance, you might seek big visions and just be given endless hints of your own lack of skills and bad attitudes toward the task. After you learn more of the process and find even your seeking is given to you, then your seeking will have become wise. That is, you will be given to seek what is ready to be given. You are also then well into the path of regeneration that Swedenborg describes. But, you might say, suppose one person gets into this process and gets endless social understanding and nothing of heaven or God? I would not complain. What is of God and heaven this person is seeing as social. Heaven, where the joy of one is the joy of all, is terribly social. I am saying that the inward process can be understood in many frames of reference, and I don't know that one is really superior to the others. The discoveries of uses will all focus around becoming ever more useful and doing the highest with the gifts one has been given. The same process in its full outer and inner aspects makes a master bricklayer, as well as a considerate person, and even the religiously enlightened. In a way, it is wrong to rank one superior to the other. This only reveals your own biases. Somewhere in creation we need the impaired person who can only sweep the floor well. If this is the highest given to him to do, then this is his ticket through all the heavens. For one thing, I remind you, we need a method good for all people at any level of giftedness. For another, I am saying doing uses like baking bread is not simply a way of focusing outwardly while tripping out inwardly. The process is literally contained in the use performed. Or, more precisely, the process is contained in the attempt to be of use. There is a world of difference between simply sweeping the floor so it is swept, and sweeping as an effort to reach out and improve things, sweeping as a devotional speaking to the highest one can conceive of. If I am sweeping just to get done with the dirt on the floor, that is all that will be accomplished. Sweeping as a reaching out, seeking, will meet in the internals of the process itself the response to my seeking. I would also emphasize that the amount found is in direct relation to the seeking. Seek little, find little. Look for everything in the sweeping and, by golly, it is there. I have complete confidence in the total power of this method. But you will have to explore it to gain an equal confidence. Is the method perhaps more suited to the limited of gift than to very intelligent persons? It is suitable equally to both. To the limited it gives a concrete means to address All There Is. Its wonder for the intelligent is that it tends to bypass the falsity, intellectualisms and wonderful self-deception possible to the intelligent, because it anchors in the reality of something of use. Should we all sweep floors? It wouldn't hurt, but the greatest wonders of uses will be discovered when you come into your highest uses. Then the deepest loves can be expressed and heaven becomes very obvious. What use to perform? Look around you. What needs to be done? If you don't know your highest use, it can be found eventually while exploring uses in whatever needs to be done. You are nearing the highest use when you come on uses you can hardly help performing because they give such pleasure. These uses are the high points of life. In them you have immense recall and awareness of even fine detail. You feel at home in them and could do them forever. These uses bring you into contact with the eternal. These uses are not limiting, but instead are your own way of eternally unfolding, for they are your way to All There Is.

But I have been speaking as a psychologist describing the phenomenology of the process. How does all this relate to theology? *The process is the experience of theology*. That is a rather startling idea. When Swedenborg speaks of uses being the design of creation itself, I accept him literally. But at first a use, sweeping this floor, looks less than the concerns of *theos logos*, the study of God; only because you haven't looked for God in the sweeping of the floor. I have been criticized for not emphasizing avoiding evil and doing good. I get the impression this is supposed to be a painful process of self-compulsion. To me, this seriously misunderstands what it is all about. In uses I have been speaking of nothing else but avoiding evil and doing good. But this gives good a concrete form. The process appears like self-compulsion only at first. "To be useful, I'll pick up these things and do so and so." The more you see into the process, the more pleasure there is. Soon you do a good use simply because you prefer to do and enjoy it.

> IN HEAVEN ALL WHO PERFORM USES FROM AFFECTION FOR USE, BECAUSE OF THE COMMUNION IN WHICH THEY LIVE ARE WISER AND HAPPIER THAN OTHERS; AND WITH THEM PERFORMING USES IS ACTING SINCERELY, UPRIGHTLY, JUSTLY, AND FAITHFULLY IN THE WORK PROPER TO THE CALLING OF EACH. THIS THEY CALL CHARITY . . . —*Divine Love and Wisdom* 431

Notice affection for use and the immediate reward: they are happier and wiser than others. And notice the work proper to the calling of each. Uses are the concrete acts that correspond to charity and good. The universal and even heavenly aspect of use becomes more apparent when we follow from their source in affections out to the community of good.

> . . . A MAN'S SPIRIT IS NOTHING ELSE THAN AFFECTION . . .
> —*Divine Love and Divine Wisdom* 21

. . . USES EXIST IN THE HEAVENS WITH ALL VARIETY AND DIVERSITY. THE USE OF ONE PERSON IS IN NO CASE EXACTLY LIKE THE USE OF ANOTHER; SO TOO THE PLEASURE OF ONE IS IN NO CASE EXACTLY LIKE THE PLEASURE OF ANOTHER. BEYOND THIS, THE PLEASURES OF EACH PARTICULAR USE ARE COUNTLESS . . . STILL THEY ARE CLOSELY CONNECTED IN A PATTERN, SO THAT THEY FOCUS ON EACH OTHER IN THE SAME WAY AS DO THE USES OF EACH MEMBER, ORGAN AND INNER PART OF THE BODY . . . ON THE BASIS OF THIS ALL-ENCOMPASSING AND DETAILED VIEW, THEY ACT AS ONE.

—*Heaven and Hell* 405

EACH INDIVIDUAL HAS HIS OWN PARTICULAR CONTRIBUTION. FOR EVERY COMMON USE IS MADE UP OF COUNTLESS ELEMENTS . . . ALL THESE PARTICULAR ELEMENTS, ARRANGED AND STRUCTURED ACCORDING TO THE DIVINE PATTERN AND TAKEN TOGETHER, CONSTITUTE AND COMPLETE A COMMON USE, WHICH IS A COMMON GOOD.

—*Heaven and Hell* 392

It is a short step from this to the Grand Man.

IN THE LORD'S SIGHT THE WHOLE HUMAN RACE IS AS ONE MAN, ALL THOSE IN ONE KINGDOM ARE ALSO AS ONE MAN . . . NOT THAT THE MEN THEMSELVES THUS APPEAR TOGETHER, IT IS THE USES WITH THEM THAT DO SO. THOSE MEN WHO ARE GOOD USES, THOSE, THAT IS, WHO DO USES FROM THE LORD APPEAR TOGETHER AS A MAN, COMPLETE IN FORM AND BEAUTIFUL. THESE ARE THEY WHO DO USES FOR THE SAKE OF THE USES THEMSELVES, THAT IS, WHO LOVE USES BECAUSE THEY ARE USES TO THE HOUSEHOLD, OR TO THE TOWN, OR TO THE PROVINCE OR TO THE KINGDOM, OR TO ALL MANKIND. ON THE OTHER HAND, THOSE WHO DO USES, NOT ON ACCOUNT OF THE USES, BUT ON ACCOUNT OF THEMSELVES ONLY OR THE WORLD ONLY, ALSO APPEAR IN THE LORD'S SIGHT AS A MAN, BUT A MAN DEFECTIVE AND UGLY.

—*Divine Love and Divine Wisdom* [Post.] 17

Our uses in which we participate in the common good is also the Lord acting through us.

> "BEING IN THE LORD" MEANS TO BE A USE, AND "BEING A MAN" MEANS TO DO USES FROM THE LORD TO THE NEIGHBOR FOR HIS SAKE. —*Divine Love and Divine Wisdom* 35

Uses, good, charity toward the neighbor, that you love one another. Now we have spoken of uses both for personal development and as part of spiritual development. Is it a better method for one or the other? No, for the two are really the same process. Personal development includes the near to hand necessities that prepare for the longer range experiences of the spiritual. They are part of the same continuum. The Lord may choose to emphasize the one or the other as the "language" you will understand the best.

So this is uses, a simple method for both personal and spiritual development. It applies to all human acts in which you attempt to reach outside yourself. It includes caring for yourself as an instrument to be kept in order. It includes one's occupation or calling used as a way of doing good. It is, at its heart, the same as charity, the doing good for the neighbor. Among the searches in uses is the attempt to experience one's highest use in the love of the life.

Use anchors us in a real doing of something of use while inwardly there is an infinite series of discoveries, which include how to do an act better, learning of one's own faults and traits, seeing into the general order of things and, at it highest, the experience of heaven and the Divine.

To be of use is open to all, even the most limited. The method has its own safeguards. If you overemphasize inner vision, it will bother you with your lack of outer skill.

It begins simply by looking around at what needs doing and doing it. And, in the doing, look to see what is the Lord's simple, intimate gift to you. Although it is inwardly as rich and complex as all there is, it is also as simple as sweeping the floor, very well, with a certain earnest devotion. I need not specify the right way to practice uses more than this, for if you try, you will be shown precisely in relation to your effort and what is ultimately useful for you. That is the wonder of uses.

Self-Reflection in the Forging of a Person

A THING MAY BE PRESENT TO A MAN A HUNDRED TIMES, BUT IF HE PERSISTENTLY FAILS TO NOTICE IT, IT CANNOT BE SAID TO ENTER INTO HIS EXPERIENCE. WE ARE ALL SEEING FLIES, MOTHS AND BEETLES BY THE THOUSAND, BUT TO WHOM, SAVE AN ENTOMOLOGIST, DO THEY SAY ANYTHING DISTINCT?

— William James, *Psychology*

THOUGHT IS NOTHING BUT INTERNAL SIGHT.

— Emanuel Swedenborg

THE MEDITATION OF MY HEART SHALL BE UNDERSTANDING.

— Psalms 49:3

At some time you may have wanted a room separate from others: a small place—high, overlooking people, cars and things of the world. It would be a place to rest and reconsider one's life. Let us build such a place—a place made for reflecting on what concerns one and equally a place for dreaming. The height of your sanctuary above the street . . . stores . . . people . . . world will depend upon you. Some will build it not far from the streets. Others will make a sanctuary that looks down upon all the worlds. The sanctuary is self-reflection.

We will reflect on self-reflection so that you might consider whether you wish to fashion such a place, above the world.

Years ago, after a difficult day, I went for an evening walk. The streets were empty, darkness and shadows softened all forms, a cricket's chirp seemed friendly. I thought to myself, what a contrast between the day's stresses and the peace of evening. It suddenly struck me that I was free to come back every evening. No matter how bad things got, I could come back to this place of rest. I was a boy then. Since then, as a psychologist, I have explored psychoanalysis, dreams, fantasy, hypnosis, meditation, all the various exotic-sounding ways of peeking into the mind. Each lost its wonder after awhile. Yet I still come back to the same kind of peaceful reflection I found as a boy. Since then it has grown in depth and wonder. I've looked at rusted machinery for an hour and come away with a feeling for rust and iron, and a host of little lessons learned. I've watched people go by for hours in wonder and amazement at the parade of human differences. I've learned to gaze at anything, pose questions, and see it slowly answer my questions. Later I learned writing from freely setting down what I found.

Self-reflection is extremely simple and subtly complicated. Under the term introspection it was long ago dismissed by scientific psychology as too unreliable to be worth investigating. Under the terms contemplation or meditation it has played a major role in most religions. In the oriental religions meditation was developed into a fine and very difficult art to obtain unusual states of awareness as in yoga. Our concern here is with basic self-reflection, for it is the most immediately useful. I would like to show many sides of it so that you might consider it for yourself. It is richest when you have leisure time, time to spend. It may be easiest in the early morning or in the evening. Usually there is an inner calling, a concern, a problem, a question or just a vague feeling that calls one. It is as though one feels called upon to look, to feel, to assess. If this is done leisurely, almost without plan or compulsion, in response to an inner calling, the results are the richest. It's the very opposite of doing something like a job because it has to be done. It should be like play, like an infant slowly exploring pots and pans for the first time. The pots and pans of later life are whatever interests or concerns one wishes to explore.

The most critical question is what to reflect upon. One could, in an uptight way, grab at likely subjects such as how to get better grades, or get along with parents, etc. The most productive self-reflection works on whatever is uppermost. This will need some explaining. One evening I am fresh from a fight with a superior at work. It is difficult to think of anything else. I feel like examining all sides of this situation. This was uppermost. On a number of evenings I surveyed my opinions and decided what my values were. Sometimes I'll have a dream or a vague feeling that is gone over. The focus may be simply, "What on earth do I feel now?" The uppermost concern is like the top piece of business on the pile. The top concern is what one can focus on and stay with for a while. It wants doing. Usually after fifteen minutes of pondering and writing, one finds that the concern has resolved itself and graduated to a deeper understanding. One implication of this is that this concern in the forefront can be of any nature from the vaguest feeling to "Is there a God?" It need not even make sense. I can conceive of a person feeling like writing nonsense, and seriously sit down, write nonsense and then consider its implications for him. There should be no preset limits to the subject matter of self-reflection. Anything is game as long as it reflects the fabric of your existence. In my journal of self-reflections there is absolutely nothing I might not consider; aches and pains, sex, death, God, my faults, my greatness, ghosts, the unreal, or the vaguest of feelings and slipperiest of ideas.

There is a deeper aspect to this kind of self-reflection. It should combine the highest and lowest powers of mind. When I used the analogy of the room high above the streets, I was implying the highest aspect of mind. At this level, mind permits itself to reflect upon itself that it might see and judge of itself. This is, for me, another dimension of existence in which the person can consider and even reconsider his existence and judge it, and even alter his choices. At this level, mind or one's existence becomes aware of and judges and chooses itself. There is a lower aspect to mind too. At its best, self-reflection, the highest aspect of mind, takes account of its lower aspects.

By low aspects, I am referring to a host of vague subjective phenomena, feelings, anxieties, dreams, fantasies, weird notions, etc. These are more primitive in that they are half-formed, strange, upwellings that may well not make any sense to consciousness. The highest function of self-reflection should also take account of, begin with, explore, and—eventually—judge the lowest aspects of mind. This kind of self-reflection is very different from the published works on philosophy in which a brilliant mind remains on the level of thinking or rationalizing. The following is an example of self-reflection that begins at this primitive level.

> In the midst of reading, an image came to mind. Though I was reading of earthquakes at sea, the image was entirely unrelated. I saw a scene in a medieval French drama, a terrace outside a mansion, a French courtyard with the feeling of a small French town. Another, older scene, I keep seeing a courtyard near a factory at the beginning of the industrial revolution. It is empty, sunny, feeling of great peace and leisure. The theme in both scenes is leisure, pleasure, which is what I am doing now. I'm in my bunk, warm under a wool blanket. Nothing to do. Savor, enjoy. Again I see everything is an image of everything else. Because I now choose to enjoy leisure, pleasure, I recall scenes of the same nature.

It was many years before I came to the idea of writing down these gems of self-reflection. When I thought of it, I discovered that most of the best ideas that bobbed to the surface of my mind sank again and were lost in minutes. I found a good notebook and started setting down my ideas. It was as though a whole process that was casual and not too important took on importance. What was a temporary, soon-lost process became permanent. The very reality of vague feelings and half-felt truths that rose near consciousness was strengthened and affirmed by setting them down. My journal was the place I met myself and took myself seriously. The idea of a written journal came from Gabriel Marcel.[1] I could see this great French philosopher was simply, persis-

1. Marcel, Gabriel. *Presence and Immorality*. Pittsburgh: Duquesne University Press, 1967. A great French thinker shares his journal, examining life in general and his own life in particular.

tently trying to understand one idea at a time by painstakingly analyzing himself. For instance, he did a volume on the mystery of being a person.[2] He had to look at his own life to gradually open all the unknowns in this experience. I am personally convinced there are whole areas of human experience that have never been explored yet.[3] Feeling especially acquires reality when set down. Perhaps the journal only comes later, when one realizes that one's own reflections are worth something to one's self.

Clearly the journal should not be written for anyone else. That would constrict it. The journal is an encounter with one's self. It need not be well written. It need not even make sense to others. It is free ground, ground on which I can wrestle with and consider myself, or my feelings of the world, or analyze feeling itself, or take apart my mind, or consider my toenails if I choose to. It is not for others. If, like Gabriel Marcel's Journal it is of use to others, fine. If it is not, that is OK too.

If nothing else, I see the style of the journal as removing all the restrictions on writing. It is not penned for others, or for a term paper. *Yah mach ich fosthic!* I can say anything I please. It is as free as I permit. In part, I seem to find that this very free self-expression aids my writing. I believe that this kind of free expression, unlimbering the mind, freeing tongue and pen, can aid one to become a creative writer. Though this may be one result, it is not the main aim.

My real aim is to understand everything. Though I am small, and not too wise, and no one believes I can do it—for $1.00, I can get pen and paper and attempt it. In the end, only I will judge its use. It is a most serious and grand enterprise. Yet it takes only pen, paper and maybe fifteen to thirty minutes every other day . . . or maybe every day. Since you will be boss of your enterprise you do it as you wish. I can only suggest by my own experience. I've done best by writing a bit every day.

---

2. Marcel, Gabriel. *The Philosophy of Existence*. London: Harvill, 1948. Self-reflections on the mystery of being human.

3. In Carl Rogers and Barry Stevens (Eds.), *Person to Person: The Problem of Being Human*. Walnut Creek, Calif.: Real People Press, 1967. See pages 214ff., which explore a whole series of inner experiences into images, trance-like states, dreams, and mental illness. The loss of ego awareness and ego enlightenment are also considered.

I may be bored or tired and then sit down and study the inside of boredom or tiredness itself. The encounter with myself is friendly, pleasant, sometimes a little frightening. It clarifies where I am and where I am going. Self-reflection should have some heroic quality, like a giant testing his own strength. It should venture into areas of thought and feeling seldom visited by others. It should attack the very basis of one's existence. It can question or examine anything.

Self-reflection is likely to revolve around several major areas, though this is so free an enterprise other areas could be devised. A key area is the study of feelings, anxieties, dreams, fantasies or any subjective experiences. It is important, also, to stand back from these and indicate what they show of you or how they fit with your life. This latter step is critical or the subjective becomes a forest of possibilities in which one is soon lost. Some may want to question the very basis and nature of thought or experience itself. Sometimes you will be examining your values, what matters most to you or where you take a stand. Especially when having troubles with others, it would be well to examine your own reactions, attempt to formulate their position and set an appropriate course of action. Some will want to examine major issues such as war, love, politics, religion, etc. In these areas it would be well to try to get at your own feeling-values to formulate your position. Occasionally, the scholarly or philosophical person will study a special interest such as art or language by considering the area through his own experiences.

Examples will clarify what is meant. The following begins with a fringe experience in which I try to describe just how my face felt. It leads, unexpectedly, to the discovery of a major personal trait. My judgment of the trait ends it. There were several entries leading to this one, with the trends in the others clarified by this.

> My face, a mask of concern, worry, as though I seriously bore in and try to penetrate things. I could act carefree, but I don't choose to. My usual set is boring, penetrating concern to do what is right, best, perfect. Be a nice guy, Do your duties. Be so good no one can criticize. Sacrifice yourself first.

> If I choose such a set, what reasons would I have? Well, in the first place, it seems defensive. Be so damn good no one can criticize. Yet they criticize me as being no fun, a worry wart, which is correct. It is a prideful position, prideful over those who are not neat, punctual, doing things right. When I look at my do good style it must be a pain in the ass to others! No wonder I have headaches. It delegates poorly ("others won't do as well as I do"). And it sure is a pain to me.

What commends such a style? I'm hard put to find anything. It wears me down and is unpleasant to others. It does little to protect from criticism and in part awakens it. I guess its greatest value to me is that I can feel, damn it, I tried. But this is somewhat like a plea to Nameless Fate and Fate is not obliged to respond.

The following came after a visit to Karachi, Pakistan. The great poverty of the people bothered me. In Pakistan, Allah is God and I felt a little angry at Allah. The entry is an effort to resolve this discomfort. It succeeds partially.

> Two days of battling with language and money differences. Today I feel a sort of spiritual indigestion. The root of it is this terrible poverty. Here I was a rich man able to give away rupees. Dirty kids, unwashed ragged clothes, no sidewalks, dirt, burlap hovels for homes. I visited a Moslem temple with mixed feelings. Rode a camel and felt a sudden burst of anger at Allah who keeps his people so poor.
>
> I think a man has the right and indeed, the obligation to question the works of Allah. But there is an equal obligation to try to see the use in what Allah does. I see a kind of alien, foreign, justice buried in poverty. This, by no means makes it right that it continue. Poverty wastes nothing, except people. In poverty everything is used. What man leaves, birds and insects eat. And what animals leave, time eats. And Allah eats time itself like a tidbit.

The following came after having constant trouble with a superior at work. In a long preamble I analyzed his traits, but then decided there was something more I could learn from the situation.

> More trouble with the chief mate today. It teaches me not to try to be the good guy with everyone. I am better off getting angry at him. Deeper—it teaches me to detach from interdependence on the opinions of some others. I'll never please him so to hell with him. Detach, so that in my life space I am stable and safe. It is my fault if I let him spoil my day. General Dictum—detach from those with whom there is no compatibility.

The next entry illustrates self-reflection on borderline experiences leading to the experience of a trend which is the opposite of my usual consciousness. Again, the general direction was unclear until I had arrived.

> There is a puzzling fringe to my present trend. Whatever I am doing, looking at my hand, listening to the clock tick, etc. it says. "No, not there." This internal director pulls me away from the track, but towards what I don't know. I have a hunch that—an idea so vague it escapes me. It pulls me away from *any track!* Good heavens, I'll lose conscious direction! It leads me away from any fixity. I could, for instance, put my feet up on the desk and just stare at the wall. That would be OK to this new director. *Tracklessness*. It also would relieve me of all cares. It takes me away from things, from duties, from all must do's. It will accept any passing fantasy, or intuition or memory, willy nilly, come what may. Of course, at the moment I am tracking tracklessness! With it, comes all kinds of memories of times I did as I pleased. This tracklessness is a relief because I am so duty bound. In a way it seems like the polar opposite of my consciousness.
>
> Consciousness—I must do my duties, get ahead, not waste time—burden.

> Other pole—drift, pin to nothing, do nothing, scatter, what the hell. Relief. Nothing to be done.

The reader may have sensed this is a kind of self-analysis. Indeed, successful self-analyses have proceeded in this way. This kind of process serves a number of functions. It studies, throws light on, and records any area of human experience. It may give life and substance to feelings or areas of human experience that are generally unknown or unrecognized. It clarifies what one believes and chooses. It forges a person.

For me a person, as distinguished from an average anybody, is one who has a distinctive style. He has reflected on his style. He can describe himself as others see him. He knows himself. Moreover, after reflection he has chosen to be as he is. He has a position. He takes a stand. He is unique, an individual. When I understand him, his style, his stand, his whole world is of one piece. It makes sense. He is not just a messy copy of others opinions and ways. Such a person is interesting, like a complex drama having running through it a rich thread of meaning. Self-reflection is the forging of this kind of individuality.

What is self-reflection? Awareness reaching round and in itself, searching its direction, its purpose, its source. It lies between and is higher than most psychology and philosophy. I consider this self-reflection one of the highest and most useful things a person can do. It raises a life of simply doing and responding to things, to life imaging and judging itself. If nothing else, it makes use of all the subjective fringe of mind. It clarifies personal values. It enables one to judge and to plan. In my mind's eye I can see a place in which the whole of existence views itself, reflects on itself, becomes Aware of What Is. This is the place in the world, above all the worlds.

If your journal lasts long enough to go into several volumes, you will discover that a few basic themes underlie all of it. Moreover, these themes spiral around the root theme of your whole life. The root theme is often so universal, touching upon all things at once, as to be difficult to describe. It is as though all of life is a spiral searching its own core, and in the center is a peace that encompasses all and asks nothing further.

Exploring Swedenborg's Dream Journal

> IF THERE IS A PROPHET AMONG YOU, I THE LORD MAKE MYSELF KNOWN TO HIM IN A VISION, I SPEAK WITH HIM IN A DREAM.
>
> — (Num. 12:6)

Dreams are a personal process that need to be understood in a personal way. For a long while I felt that Swedenborg's private *Journal of Dreams* was too raw a material for a general audience to use. When I learned that the Swedenborg Foundation intended to reprint this *Journal,* I boldly proposed to do a commentary. But when it came right down to the task, I had misgivings that bear directly on the nature of dreams and how they can finally be understood and used.

Once you get used to the peculiar language of dreams they become a personal guidance system with a superior overview of the nature of one's own life. As a clinical psychologist, understanding my own dreams is a prerequisite for working on a client's dreams. Before I started on Swedenborg's dreams, I required that I regain facility with my own dreams—I feel I have no right to play the expert with someone else's dreams unless I am able to understand my own. But there is a deeper reason for this self-imposed requirement. As you will see better later, dreams are a valuable guidance system. Should I be in error with

Swedenborg's dreams, I would expect my personal guidance system to tell me so. I need my own dreams to monitor my understanding of his. This might surprise you. But when you are working on something, especially when it is close to your life concerns, your dreams will tell you how well you are doing. We will see several instances in which Swedenborg felt that his own dreams were commenting on the writing then concerning him.

C. G. Jung, the noted analytical psychologist, said dreams are objective, that is they come from a level more objective than one's subjective point or view. Here's an example: as I was finishing my Ph.D. dissertation, *Mind in Hyperspace*,[1] I felt I had made an immense contribution to science. After all, I had added the fifth, sixth, and seventh dimensions to real space. I remember quite well that my dreams said in effect, well it's pretty good, but definitely dull! This comment dampened my enthusiasm, but one learns to appreciate the fact that dreams come from a higher, more objective viewpoint. This is why I am watching my own guidance system while commenting on Swedenborg's dreams.

Why comment on Swedenborg's *Journal?* A great deal occurs in this *Journal*. It goes far beyond a dull listing of someone's peculiar fancies. It may be the oldest long series of dreams in existence; it is also the product of a great mind. And, most fortunate of all, it came just at the time that Swedenborg, the renowned scientist, was becoming Swedenborg the spirit seer. We will see the inner struggles and processes of a man coming into accord with the will of God. If I could ask for the dreams of any period in his life, this is precisely the period I would ask for.

But dreams are in a rather arcane language. If you haven't worked with your own dreams, they easily seem to be a mishmash of elements into which one could read most anything. Swedenborg's heirs tore a few pages of dreams out of an earlier journal that presumably appeared scandalous to them. I warrant they had no experience with their own

1. W. Van Dusen, "Mind in Hyperspace," Ph.D. dissertation. University of Ottawa, University Microfilms, Ann Arbor, MI, 1959.

dreams. Some translators omitted certain sexual dreams altogether[2] or translated them into Latin.[3] Others concluded that Swedenborg must be mad. I am quite sure these pundits weren't looking at the weird mishmash in their own dreams! We will be looking at all of the dreams available. Very simply I feel a commentary is needed to help the reader understand what is going on—this way, the untranslated dreams are turned into something of use to others.

Suppose this personal and private journal had not long ago fallen into public hands. If I were handed the original journal and asked if it should be made public now, for the first time, I'd agonize over the question. After all, if Swedenborg were alive there would be no question in my mind but that he'd have to okay publication, and my guess is he would not okay it, feeling that it was too much of him and too little of the spiritual world. With Swedenborg gone from the world, my vote would be to suppress it until a competent commentary could be made. My reason—the *Journal* is too personal, too raw, and open to too many interpretations. I feel we have no right to peek into the corners of someone else's life without their permission. in the case of a person who has left this world, I would feel we have no right to publish *unless* the material is to be treated respectfully and made of some public use. In spite of the current trend of the media to exploit even the most distorted peeks into the private lives of famous people, I don't feel we have the right to peek even if it is printed and put before us. As a psychotherapist I've had to look closely at the personal details of many lives, but only when asked to do so, and for the purpose of helping the person. The therapist's intent is so different from the sensationalist's peek. So this, too—avoiding sensationalist

---

2. R. L. Tafel, *Documents Concerning Swedenborg*, Swedenborg Society, London, 1890, Vol. 2, pp. 134ff. This translation of the *Journal of Dreams* has deliberate omissions of parts with sexual content.

3. C. Th. Odhner, *Journal of Dreams*, Academy Book Room, Bryn Athyn, PA, 1918. This English version translated the sexual sections from Swedish into Latin.

The version used by Van Dusen in his commentary volume is the translation of J. J. G. Wilkinson, edited by William Ross Woofenden, the only complete English rendition. A second edition of this version with many additional footnotes was published in 1989 by the Swedenborg Scientific Association, Bryn Athyn, PA.

exploitation—was behind my offer to do a commentary. We will look at all the dreams and experiences and try to understand them. My intent is neither to build up nor to tear down Swedenborg, but only to learn as much as we can from this material. I cannot be Swedenborg's therapist, but perhaps we can all learn something—it is this attempt to learn that gives us some right to look at such personal material.

What Is A Dream?

Dreams are a spontaneous and natural process in which the central life concerns of an individual are presented in a dramatic language of correspondences. Let me elaborate on this. *It is a spontaneous and natural process* because it occurs in everyone whether they have any interest in dreams or not. It appears to occur in animals too, though we can't ask them to confirm this. It begins in the womb and occurs throughout life. It must be natural, because it occurs without our bidding. Dreams are of the *central life concerns*. We have to penetrate their language to see that they carry a message of this importance.

Dreams are in a dramatic language of correspondences. The idea of correspondences comes from Swedenborg, and indeed his dreams may well have been the beginning of his direct experience with this language. Swedenborg says our facial expressions represent our feelings within. When the expression accurately reflects the life within, it *corresponds* to it.[4] The idea of correspondences enabled Swedenborg to deal with different but corresponding levels of reality simultaneously. The dream images correspond to truths and qualities in the inner life. It is as though the source of dreams can only speak a dramatic language of things and events that represent its inner quality and nature. To me this says something very profound about the source of dreams. If I am mistaken in a relationship to another person, why can't dreams just say, "Van, you are wrong about so and so. He is finer than you realize?" Although occasionally there is speech in dreams, dreams are mostly composed of dramatic visual representations. The struggles of a dreamer

4. E. Swedenborg, *Apocalypse Explained*, Swedenborg Foundation, New York, 1972, paragraph 1080.

even to understand these images says immediately that they are not from the dreamer's usual sphere of thought and language. There have been efforts to teach the dream process to speak plain English. They have been only partly successful. Whatever we are dealing with in dreams, its natural mode of thought is this dramatic language of correspondences—dramatic because it is inclined to make statements by showing actual incidents involving us. It speaks in terms of dramatic events which correspond to elements in the inner life and the experience of the person.

Let me show you a short dream. I taught dream interpretation to a group of mental health workers. We had a social-scientist intern in the group. He presented a dream in which there was a hut full of food. In the upper story an animal was gnawing at something. I learned from prior work that the dreamer accidentally enacts a dream while telling it. By watching the dreamer's gestures while he is telling it you can sometimes see some of the meaning. When the social scientist said "hut full of food" he held his hands out to just the width of his body. He was quite stout. So I held my hands out to the same width and said, "I wonder where there is a hut full of food this wide." He smiled and said, "Oh I see that. But what is this gnawing in the upper story?" I paraphrased the dream. Pointing to him I said, "in the upper story a gnawing is going on." It took just a few moments trying to get at the quality of gnawing for him to see that it corresponded to his constant worrying about things. He was reluctant to speak of his worries, but we didn't need that. He now knew the dream was an image of his life. The image was rather unflattering, as is often true of dreams. The dream said, in effect, you are like a primitive dwelling place (hut), you eat too much, and you worry all the time. Because the dream connected "hut full of food" and "gnawing in the upper story," one could suspect that his excess eating was related to his worrying. But this is speculation on our part—he would have to confirm it. At first the dream just seemed peculiar. "Why would I dream of a hut full of food?" he asked. Once he had connected it to his body he had the key to working out the other detail, the gnawing in the upper story.

Why does the Dream Maker speak this odd language of correspondence? We don't really know. My experience strongly suggests that this is the natural language of the Dream Maker. Perhaps one value of it is that it leaves the dreamer free. If this man's dream simply said you eat too much and worry too much, it would be a disturbing insult. Instead it presents a curious incident he can try to figure out or not, as he wishes. It seems to leave his will free. I also think the Dream Maker is in a position to know all the memories, experiences, hopes, and fears of the dreamer. It must be at the very center of the life.

I coined the term Dream Maker just to avoid disputes as to who or what fashions the dream. We know this much: dreaming is a universal process, occurring in all persons. It has its own language, which is highly symbolic or, even better described in Swedenborg's own terms, is a language of correspondences. Dreams are apparently fully aware of the most intimate details and memories of the individual's life. The Dream Maker chooses to comment on the life. The reader may need more experience to see that this commentary is from a more objective viewpoint than the dreamer's own personal view. In the above-mentioned dream incident, the man considered himself of average build. He looked fat to everyone around him and to the Dream Maker. The Dream Maker chooses to comment in his own language on the quality of the life. If I could put in a single phrase what the concern of the Dream Maker is, I would say definitely *the quality of the life*. When life-quality is not so good, it says so. Dreams also note the individual's deepest struggles and can, at times, help the person in the clearest way. But throughout all this, this peculiar language, which we must struggle to penetrate, consistently sets dreams apart from simply an extension of the ordinary conscious life of the person—that, and their loftier, more objective viewpoint. All this is my experience. It is not "science" since no strict measures were made and no manipulation of variables has been attempted. I would also like to say that, in general, those who have worked some while at the analysis of dreams are generally in accord with each other. The great differences between Freudians and other "isms" of dreams have largely disappeared. Small differences remain, but for the most part, those with experience in dream interpretation are seeing things largely the same way regardless of their backgrounds! I'll leave the issue of what the Dream Maker is until after we have journeyed through Swedenborg's dreams. I delay addressing this central issue because the answer will begin to be apparent to you as you see Swedenborg struggling with the Dream Maker.

There has been a fairly recent discovery that has opened dreams to scientific study. It was found that when a person dreams, there are rapid eye movements (REM)—when a person dreams, you can see their eyes move around under their eyelids as they look around in their dream. First it was confirmed that REM means dreaming. Sensors were put on the eyelids to detect movement. When wakened during REM the subject would report a dream. When wakened when there was no REM, there was no dream either. Once we had a physical correlate of dreaming, then numbers of other matters were relatively simple to research. As a result we now know that the average adult has eight dreams a night. Infants dream a great deal, and there is a gradual falling off of dream frequency with age. Certain drugs suppress dreaming and others may stimulate it.

A striking discovery was made when persons were deprived of dreaming. They were allowed to sleep a normal amount of time but were awakened at the beginning of every REM. In this way they got a normal amount of sleep, but no dreams. It didn't take long for this practice to produce highly disturbed and even psychotic people, because they began dreaming even when awake. So it appears dreams are not only natural, but somehow necessary. This necessity is unrelated to any interpretation of or even awareness of the dream. The full implication of this is still unclear. It is my guess that dreams are a psychophysical necessity—that is, physically dreams are some sort of balancing or adjustment in the brain/mind itself. On a psychic level there is some sort of necessity to review and assess the life beyond the level of consciousness itself. It is as though it is necessary to come into contact with something higher in ourselves, even if we are not aware of it. Many are inclined to believe that consciousness is everything, but in dream study we come face to face with a process that goes on regardless of conscious cooperation! Those who say dreaming is merely neurons firing have surely not looked at the intelligence reflected in the process, an intelligence that uses language and concepts which routinely transcend the individual's understanding.

Another key to understanding dreams is that there are dreams of different length or importance. There are little dreams of seeming little consequence. There are dreams of average importance. And there are *big* dreams.

For instance, almost any kind of discomfort, or even outside stimuli can stimulate a dream. A person might fall asleep with his head on one arm and dream that while driving, his car became caught and crushed under a heavy beam. When he awakens and gets his heavy head off his arm, the beam is removed. This looks like a small dream. It has no major life elements. But of course there might be something in the kind of car, the beam, and how he reacted while caught. Or perhaps there is something in the fact that the dream is backwards (head on arm or beam is represented by beam on the head!).

There are also big dreams. They feel big and important when you have them. Often they reflect major discoveries or even turning points in the life. We will see in Swedenborg's series many big dreams. I'll tell you one of mine.

Background—I was a doctoral student in a Catholic university because they had the quality of training I wanted. Yet I was not Catholic, and, indeed, though widely read in religion, I had not joined any religion.

The Dream—I was walking up a low hill. It was a time of celebration because there were poles all along the way with gay colored flags. It was bright and sunny. Suddenly I was stunned to see Christ, a jet black figure on a jet black Cross. The Cross was lower to the ground than all the crosses I had seen before, and Christ was slumped over much more than any representation I had ever seen before. I knew beyond doubt this was Christ and this was Golgotha, the hill of crucifixion. A voice said, "He is well worth believing in."

Feeling and Associations—I was awakened with an awed, stunned feeling. I knew it meant it was time I commit myself openly to religion. It surprised me how much feeling I had in the dream for Christianity because I felt closer to Hinduism and Buddhism at that time. I felt I had seen the crucifixion. The dream had odd changes from the free gaiety of the sunny day of celebration, to the *black* crucifixion, to the comforting last statement. The black Cross and Christ indicated to me I had looked into something beyond ordinary human experience.

That is a big dream. It occurred 32 years ago and is still clear and powerful. I have met clients with big dreams. They are often carried around for years like a sacred treasure rarely shared. These people are often afraid to tell about them because they fear others will fail to respect and understand the power they feel. They are easy to understand if you respect the feelings and inner wisdom of the dreamer.

A frequent question that arises when I speak of dreams in a group is, what does it mean when a person has a repetitive dream? The repetitive dream is a vital message repeated over and over. Even a little effort to understand it breaks the repetition. It is the simplest of all emotional problems to solve.

The Process of Finding the Meaning of a Dream

Just for a moment let us pretend that someone has presented me with a dream to work out. The person often tells the dream as though I should be able to whip out a brilliant interpretation in a moment. Actually I can't. I usually have not even a glimmer of what it means. But I know in that person are the experiences, the associations, the life on which the dream is based. My first task is to intensify the dream, to get the person back into it, living it. I have him tell the dream again, slowly. This time I watch him closely for signs that he is enacting the dream. I inquire about his feelings. I get feeling details, that is, I ask "What did it feel like when . . . ?" I am trying to make the dream a living experience again. For a long dream I may simply pause and then say, "Where are you now in the dream?" He is in some part of a long dream. I want to start where he is. Often he will say, "I was doing so and so." It is this element which asks to come clear first. Sometimes I can ask directly, "How is that like your life?" and they relate immediately how they sense that part in their lives. These connections are usually surprises to me. I don't have brilliant foresight of what they will find. *I have only a method to help them find what the dreams say to them.*

Oftentimes the dreamer can relate the things *he does* in the dream to what *he does in life*. It's all those other odd objects and people in his dream he doesn't understand. In these cases I try to get them to pretend he is the other object or person and tell the dream from that standpoint. If he dreams about an encounter with a robber, I'll say, "Pretend now you are the robber and tell it from this viewpoint." Often he gets clues as to what the robber is in them.

With this kind of work we can often find several connections between the dream and the person's life. It is not necessary to find all the connections if there isn't time. I sometimes suggest that if the dreamer will reflect a little on the dream's connections during the day, he will find the rest of the meanings—and he does.

I want to get across the basic nature of the process: the therapist usually has little or no notion what a dream means—instead he has methods for getting the meaning from the dreamer. This is so true that I finally decided that the only valid interpretation of a dream was that which the dreamer himself or herself gives to it. Sometimes this can be disappointing. A client and I would work together some while and have what looked like several rich clues and understandings. Yet one could see them one by one disappearing from consciousness. If I finally asked, "Now what does the dream mean to you?" I'd get some simple statement that overlooked most of our discoveries. But this is to be expected. The dream language and conception transcend our understanding. People who have little experience working with this rich and transcending language are especially prone to lose it just after seeming to find it. Again this says we are dealing with processes which transcend the slim little consciousness.

I want to add another caution. When I worked with a group of mental health professionals on dream interpretation, a particular kind of misinterpretation was common. After someone recounted a dream, often someone else would think he knew what it meant and would try to force the dreamer to accept his wonderful insight. It is easy to project our interpretation onto the dreamer. In fact I could present any dream and have everyone in the group interpret it and come out with a different interpretation for each interpreter. This has been done with myths too. Present a myth and have each person find his meaning for it. There would be some similarities in these interpretations but many differences. People who haven't ever worked with their own dreams often feel particularly experts with others' dreams! Just as an example, a woman who was considering suicide had a fantasy in which she climbed inside a snow bank. All of the other "experts" in the room thought this was suicidal. But when we looked at the woman's own feelings, this was a place for recovery away from people. She felt warm and cozy in there, that is, the snow made her feel how warm (alive) she was! For her it was a quiet, cozy retreat that shut everyone else out. Because of this positive value, I encouraged her to return in fantasy to this retreat whenever she wanted. We had to find out what her dream meant to her to understand it.

In my experience strangers are particularly prone to tangle themselves in others' sexual experiences, to project themselves into sexual dreams. I sometimes left details of a sexual history out of medical records because the staff would eagerly read these details and they would not pay attention to any other part of a psychiatric history. So I just say, beware of projecting fantasies into someone else's life. Perhaps it was a good idea to leave out Swedenborg's sexual dreams in earlier generations, but now let us hope we can be a little wiser.

Perhaps now you can understand my major hesitation to comment on Swedenborg's dreams: I don't have Swedenborg to work with. That I would enjoy. I'm quite sure that our work together would discover a great deal more than I will be able to see here. This situation would be nearly impossible except for several facts that make even the absent Swedenborg's dreams clearer. We have an abundance of his own associations. He often says what a dream reminds him of or means to him. His associations and meanings are valuable clues—I will be somewhat governed by these, for I really feel the dreamer is closer to the source and wisdom in a dream than I am!

There is another saving grace in interpreting this *Journal:* we have a relatively long series of dreams and experiences. We may miss on one, but we will eventually understand themes that recur. We will see patterns in a series which we might overlook if we had only one dream.

There is another help in this series. We have not only dreams but also other kinds of experiences reported by Swedenborg. They all issued from the same life and were other aspects of what was happening. Moreover we know a great deal of Swedenborg's history before and after this series. Some purists might think we should deal with dreams alone, but that would be foolish, for it is actually the whole life that concerns us. It is a real boon to see his dream struggles in relation to what he was to become.

Yet with all these saving graces I must respect the fact that I am working within the real limitation that Swedenborg is not here to affirm or deny. I am not permitted the relationship that enables dream elements to show their meaning. So I cannot be complete, or final, or reveal all that is here. Often you will notice that I am unsure, struggling with possible meanings. That is part of the situation. My role then is to try to throw more light on what is here than you might find on your own. But in a real sense, the only final word on the meanings here is Swedenborg's life itself and its effect on history.

Meditation

I HAVE NOW BEEN IN CONVERSATION WITH SPIRITS AND ANGELS CONCERNING REFLECTION, TO WHICH I DO NOT KNOW WHETHER MEN HAVE PAID SUFFICIENT ATTENTION. IF THEY DO ATTEND TO THIS THEY WILL FIND THAT THERE ARE MORE ARCANA IN THE DOCTRINE OF REFLECTION THAN IN ANY OTHER WHATSOEVER.

— *Spiritual Diary* 733

. . . WHEN [MAN] IS IN AFFECTION FOR UNDERSTANDING, AND THROUGH THAT COMES INTO PERCEPTION OF TRUTH, HE IS THEN IN THE THOUGHT OF HIS SPIRIT, WHICH IS MEDITATION.

— *Divine Love and Wisdom* 408.8

Swedenborg meditated, and the writings* speak strongly in favor of this practice which is almost universal among religions. Yet many followers of his writings often know nothing of meditation, misunderstanding it, or even consider it dangerous. We would like to correct misunderstandings in this area, for meditation is one of the keys to regeneration.

* "The writings" are commonly used by Swedenborgians to refer to Swedenborg's complete theological works.

In terms of the writings, meditation is basically a way of opening up, experiencing and learning from the internal. It is the direct opposite of preoccupation with the external, material existence or preoccupation with one's own proprium. The writings give it a central place, even though this is not so apparent; because references to it are scattered, and described under different terms in different ways. Although some know little of it, the interior spiritual aspect of mind is relatively easy to open and enjoy. Having done so, the person finds the internal is a vast, subtle realm in itself with much to teach.

The *Encyclopaedia Britannica* describes meditation as,

> profound and generally peaceful consideration of truths that are thought to have great importance in ordering and living one's life. Meditation is especially esteemed and practiced regularly by persons who have dedicated their lives to religious pursuits.[1]

This article goes on to give references to meditation in all the world's major religions. Even though the richest literature and detailing of what is to be found in meditation occurs in Buddhist and Hindu literature, it also has prominence in Christianity and Judaism. It is a simple art, available to everyone—a direct approach to the interior life. It is perhaps the extravagant faddish claims of some current groups and the public show of meditation as an occult experience[2] that frightens and puts some people off. It is easy to lose sight of the fact that Swedenborg practiced meditation and that it may be understood in terms of the writings. In the hands of others, under other names, it looks alien, yet it is not. Those who sit quietly in an empty church in silent prayer are essentially meditating. When the writings say: "if a man would but reflect he would see . . .," they are advocating meditation.

We will first examine what meditation is in its essentials, and dispose of some of the faddish claims. Then we will look at Sweden-

1. *Encyclopaedia Britannica*, 1975, Vol. VI, p. 750.
2. *Time Magazine*, Oct. 13, 1975.

borg's own approach and the very sensitive and illuminating things that the writings have to say on the matter.

The Heart of Meditation

What essentially is meditation? Its heart is the suspension of normal thought to experience influx and the interior qualities of mind. This is its main method and purpose. In Swedenborg's *Intercourse of Soul and Body* it is made clear that all mental life is given us by influx. But in normal daily activity we tend to identify with this influx, and take it over, so to speak, as though we are the formers of all our thoughts and the makers of our existence. Thought arises and it is spoken or carried into action as though we make it so. In this direction also lies proprium,* for the implication is that there is no God and no influx, only the individual acting from himself. Meditation temporarily suspends this identification and carrying into action so that the interior qualities of mental life can be experienced, so that the process of influx can be experienced. It should be immediately apparent that this is anti-proprium. Indeed, one of the major values of meditation is to lessen the influence of proprium.

Let us look more closely at an average meditation session. A man has chosen a quiet time of day to sit relaxed with gaze fixed on a point. For ten minutes or so he will suspend any mental efforts of his own. Everything comes down to the attention fixed on a point. Sensations come and go. The thought occurs that this is a foolish waste of time. The thought is not identified with and passes. Distracting noises occur which are also noted and incorporated into the fixation on a point. After a period in which the mind busily tries to distract or get him up, even the inner life begins to calm down. Soon there is the influx of ideas as though stemming from the spot. These too are noticed but not identified with. He begins to feel calmer, as though he had entered a new peaceful world. The spot turns into images which he notes are correspondences of his inner state. He has been concerned about the

* Proprium is Swedenborg's term for the sense of selfhood and especially self-guidance; it is a sense of self living from self.

quality of his ends for some days. This theme comes back as though he can now see and move within his ends. He still doesn't identify with the process. It emerges and he can watch its emerging and what it has to show. For moments he can see where his ends tend. For moments he senses the Divine working through his ends. About ten minutes have passed and he calls himself out of meditation, feeling calm and relaxed, and a little more confident that something higher is working out through him. This would be a fairly average session of a religious person who has practiced meditation for some while.

It might be considered much the same as silent prayer except for the fixed gaze. It is quite unlike simply thinking or just verbalizing a prayer. Both would tend to interfere with perceiving influx. The value of fixing the gaze is simple. The point of concentration keeps the mind at its task of watching inner processes. If the gaze wanders, the mind wanders and the delicate process of sensing influx is lost. All meditation methods use some point of focus; and, as we shall see later, the difference between different points of focus is slight.

There are basically two kinds of meditation which really join and become one. The *Britannica* definition and Swedenborg's main approach both stress an internal focus on some idea of supreme importance. For instance Swedenborg says, "One day I was meditating upon the creation of the universe" (*True Christian Religion* 76). The focus is on a particular content. The other form of meditation, just described, does not identify with any content. Instead its internal focus is on what is occurring now in mind in order to look at mental processes without any controls and without identifying with them, or being caught up in their trends. Actually, the two approaches become one. The first focuses on an assigned topic, i.e. the creation of the universe, and the second has as its topic the spontaneous operations of mind. People who have little or no experience with meditation tend to make the first approach into merely thinking about and conjuring up one's ideas about the creation of the universe. This is just thought and not meditation. To meditate on the creation of the universe one would loosely hold that focus and watch what new understanding flows in. It is higher than just thinking about a topic. We don't recommend that those new to meditation use a topic like this; they should just let the focus be whatever is occurring now. This is the more fundamental approach which unmasks inner processes. After becoming practiced in this more fundamental kind of meditation, then one can meditate on a topic as Swedenborg did and not get involved in merely thinking. Meditation is essentially a pleasant, mild exploration and, as such, one of its hallmarks is new insight, new discovery, and a whole new basis of understanding. We can give an example. I had long pondered what was really meant by the New Church and had gathered a large file of references so diverse that they had left me even more confused. While I was meditating with no given inner focus, the solution came to me as though someone had posed a forceful question, "what one thing are the writings always dealing with?" It was as though I could see all the writings as a vast panorama colored at every point with celestial hues all having the same meaning. I could see the answer was the regeneration of people. It is *New* because they are being made new, and *Church* because this is the essence of a church. I felt stunned and pleased. Here was a simple, obvious solution I had missed. But typically this kind of sudden creative solution comes in a quiet spontaneous reflection that follows much detailed work and gathering of information. One who merely thinks about a topic usually conjures all that was already known. After all the facts have been gathered and searched over, and one is still stuck, then meditation on that area of concern can open up sudden flashes of insight. Such meditation occurs even in sleep when the issues have become central to the life. We are stressing here the basic roots of meditation so the student doesn't fall into merely thinking and ennoble this by the term meditation. At its root meditation is letting the mind go, that the onlooker might watch the spontaneous panorama of delicate internal processes. It is decidedly internal learning. The religious person can much more easily experience the Divine in this state than he can in normal waking life (*Heaven and Hell* 147). It should be easy to see why. It is a relaxed, open, receptive state. The usual effects of ten minutes of meditation are to feel relaxed, refreshed and a little less presumptuous about one's self or others. Having practiced being open and receptive, one tends to remain that way.

Almost all schools and religions that use meditation advocate doing so only a few minutes a day. Even during major training, Transcendental Meditation still advocates only 20 minutes at a time, twice a day. Those who spend whole years practicing it are engaged in a heroic effort at religious development that isn't even recommended for most people. A few minutes a day, set aside to open to the interior qualities of experience, is sufficient. The only rule is to temporarily suspend control and identification with mental processes. It is not an effort at control. The effort at control undermines the process and produces a host of internal difficulties. To produce these difficulties one need only try to fix the mind on one idea or image. The usual experience is that it drifts away in a matter of seconds; the drift is noticed sometime later, and the mind is called back, only to drift away again. Even this is a useful experience, for it tends to undermine the proprial idea that we are easily masters of ourself. Thoughts, images, feelings come and go. They are not identified with or carried to exteriors. The interior source of experience is watched. *All that the writings say of the interior as against the exterior are aspects of what is found in meditation.* The interior, generative aspect of experience is opened and revealed to awareness. The mind is found to be endlessly creative and subtle. The aspect of the self that easily thinks and speaks in correspondences becomes apparent. The depths of discovery in this realm are, in my experience, apparently endless[3] just as Swedenborg said.

Conflicting Gurus on How to Do It

Once the real goal and nature of the process are seen, the conflicting claims of this and that ancient school fall into place. How should one sit, in the *zazen* position of the Buddhists? The westerner soon finds this position is nearly impossible and painful for those not accustomed to it. The position is not important. Whatever serves the inner goal can be used. To lie down, with eyes closed, may cause many to fall asleep. Most sleep can't be counted as meditation. There is too little consciousness in it! Comfort with calm alertness is needed. Any

---

3. Van Dusen, W., *The Natural Depth in Man* (New York: Harper and Row, 1972). One of the best contemporary works in this area is L. Le Shan, *How To Meditate* (New York: Bantam Books, 1975).

position that serves this is acceptable. Should eyes be open or closed? Either way. Whichever serves best for the individual, to engender a still attentiveness. Some schools claim the necessity of using a mantra which is usually a Sanskrit name or phrase given to the subject by a teacher. Endlessly and silently repeating the mantra serves to jam the verbal circuits. It is as though the mind badly needs something to focus on. The mantra gives a harmless, nondistracting inward focus. For those who want to try the same way, it will be found that counting the exhaled breaths up to ten and repeating will do the same thing, or simply counting each exhaled breath as one will do as well. The exhaled breath is identified with more than inhaled because we are more relaxed when exhaling. Various kinds of harmless, nondistracting focuses have been used; staring at an outward point, meditating on a part of the body (i.e., center of the forehead, heart beat, tip of a finger, etc.), symbolic hand positions, dance gestures, etc. Although various schools argue for the wonder of their approach over others, anything that can be used as a still point of focus will work. In church, gazing at the altar will do as well. One finds the most used approach yields so much that it begins to appear superior to all others. A focus provides a center for mind. A still sameness of the focus is necessary. Most of our external experience is of the mind in flight from experience to experience. Meditation, on whatever chosen focus, is the opposite of this flight. We are so accustomed to flitting from one thing to another that some sort of focus is particularly useful at first. As one becomes accustomed to the inner qualities of experience, these later can become the center, and no other focus is necessary. The debates about how one sits, what master so and so does, mantras, various foci, kinds of breathing, etc., are just debates which lead away from the core of the experience. Try the simplest focus, sitting comfortably gazing at a point, or any focus that works for you.

Meditation is a gentle, subtle exercise. Those who hope for strange visions and breath-taking experiences, like an exciting television program, are going to be disappointed. The greatest danger in the beginning is that one will be too impatient, expect too much, and find it a waste of time. *Until you have gotten a real sense of what the interior of human experience is like and seen processes in yourself given to you like influx, you haven't even gotten into it*. The earliest efforts have a calm, relaxing effect and this is sufficient gain for the beginning. In fact, this is why it is being used to treat tension states. Later you will have experience of the internal and become accustomed to influx. Large, very intense experiences are given occasionally only to patient long-term seekers who have already learned a great deal about how the interior of mind operates. Also, when meditation is understood inwardly, then it becomes easier to mediate anywhere, any time, in the midst of work and even in the midst of stress. It is, after all, an inner perceptiveness, and this perceptiveness is possible any time.

The major effects of meditation, put in probable order of their appearance are the following:

a) relaxation, calming, refreshing.

b) struggles with what is one's own (proprium) and what is influx.

c) drift into brief periods in which the inner opens, represents itself and then is cut off as the individual tries to seize and control this process.

d) learning of the mind's endless creativity and readiness to represent itself, correspondences.

e) physical changes such as lowered respiration, lowered blood pressure, change in brain waves.[4]

f) a gradual spiritualizing of values.

g) personal religious revelations.

I would stress that the later effects are not to be sought, because seeking impedes their appearance. One is seeking to enter and understand the inner life; that is all. It is sufficient if one simply learns how

4. Ornstein, R., *The Nature of Human Consciousness* (San Francisco: Freeman, 1973) pp. 255–274.

to relax. Meditation tends to affect the rest of the life. After a short acquaintance I can often guess if a person has meditated and for roughly how long. A peaceful centeredness to their life is what I look for. If nothing else, meditation provides a peaceful refuge. Some people tend to over-identify with their life difficulties, as though there is no other way to experience life. Meditation is a peaceful refuge away from the noises of the world, available for king and pauper alike, anywhere, any time, a refuge that gives perspective on the outer life.

Swedenborg's Meditation

The documents bearing on Swedenborg's experience give only a fragmented picture of his personal practice and experience. Yet the particular fragments can be interpreted to reveal a fairly coherent picture. There are really several interrelated processes which go under different names and yet are internally related. These are prayer (especially nonverbal and reflective prayer), reflection and meditation, the hypnogogic, trance state, and dreaming. Swedenborg knew so much of these states that I have said elsewhere that no modern literature yet compares with the depth of his discoveries.[5] All of these states bear on the internal of experience. Except for dreams, modern psychology has simply not paid as much attention to these areas as he did. Although we will focus on his meditation, the account will have bearing on his experience with all of these states. His earliest reference to meditation mentions minimal breathing while in prayer,

> THERE WAS THEN SHOWN TO ME CERTAIN SPECIES OF RESPIRATIONS. . . . I WAS FIRST ACCUSTOMED THUS TO RESPIRE IN MY EARLY CHILDHOOD, WHEN SAYING MY MORNING AND EVENING PRAYERS, AND OCCASIONALLY AFTERWARDS, WHEN EXPLORING THE HARMONIES OF THE LUNGS AND HEART, AND ESPECIALLY WHEN DEEPLY ENGAGED IN WRITING THE WORKS THAT HAVE BEEN PUBLISHED. FOR

5. Van Dusen, W., *The Presence of Other Worlds* (New York: Harper and Row, 1974).

A COURSE OF YEARS I CONTINUALLY OBSERVED THAT THERE WAS A TACIT RESPIRATION, SCARCELY PERCEPTIBLE, CONCERNING WHICH IT WAS SUBSEQUENTLY GIVEN ME TO REFLECT, AND THEN TO WRITE. I WAS THUS DURING MANY YEARS, FROM THE PERIOD OF CHILDHOOD, INTRODUCED INTO SUCH RESPIRATIONS, ESPECIALLY BY MEANS OF ABSORBING SPECULATIONS . . . AS OTHERWISE THE INTENSE STUDY OF TRUTH IS SCARCELY POSSIBLE.

— *Spiritual Diary* 3464

Anyone who thinks Swedenborg overemphasizes the importance of respiration in meditation should see the equally great emphasis in Hindu Yoga. The lessened breathing is the resultant of an intense inward concentration; inward concentration cannot be strengthened simply by breathing less. Lessened oxygen consumption is one of the clear findings with meditation.[6] Both the depth and frequency of breathing lessen. Although Swedenborg later wrote that breathing might stop, this is hardly likely. He was working alone and had no one to observe him. The implication that he was not aware of breathing is that his meditation was so intense it had passed over into trance where there is a temporary loss of all outer awareness. There is only internal awareness. In this state he experienced a panorama of visions and experiences in heaven and hell. The fact that his breathing had gotten so low means that his inward concentration was extraordinary. Likely not one in a hundred people who concentrated in prayer would have the same experience. The meaning of this is probably an unusually powerful mind which is accustomed to concentration and unusually persistent in seeking out its ends. My guess is that his earliest experience was with meditation that had a specific inner content because it was associated with seeking answers in prayer.

Yet his comments on meditation in *Rational Psychology* show experience with what Naranjo[7] now calls concentrative meditation, described above as focusing on whatever comes.

6. Ornstein, R., *The Nature of Human Consciousness*, pp. 255–274.
7. Naranjo, C., and Ornstein, R., *On the Psychology of Meditation* (New York: Viking, 1971).

> . . . WE ARE ABLE TO APPROACH NEARER AND NEARER TO THE PURE INTELLECT, DOING THIS BY MEANS OF UNIVERSAL IDEAS AND A KIND OF PASSIVE POTENCY; AND THIS, IN THAT WE REMOVE PARTICULAR IDEAS, THAT IS, WITHDRAW THE MIND FROM TERMS AND IDEAS THAT ARE BROKEN, LIMITED, AND MATERIAL, AND AT THE SAME TIME, FROM DESIRES AND LOVES THAT ARE PURELY NATURAL. THEN THE HUMAN INTELLECT, BEING AT REST FROM HETEROGENEOUS THRONGS, AS IT WERE, AND REMAINING ONLY IN ITS OWN IDEAS AND THOSE PROPER TO THE PURE INTELLECT, CAUSES OUR MIND TO UNDERGO NO OTHER CHANGES, OR TO DRAW FORTH NO OTHER REASONS SAVE THOSE THAT ARE CONCORDANT WITH THE IDEAS OF THE PURE INTELLECT. IN THIS WAY OUR INTELLECT ENJOYS INMOST REPOSE AND INMOST DELIGHT; FOR THIS CONCURRENCE THEN APPEARS AS AN INFLUX OF A CERTAIN LIGHT OF INTELLIGENCE WHICH ILLUMINATES THE WHOLE SPHERE OF THOUGHT, AND, BY A CERTAIN CONSENSUS, I KNOW NOT WHENCE, DRAWS ITS WHOLE MIND TOGETHER, AND INMOSTLY DICTATES THAT A THING IS TRUE OR GOOD, OR THAT IT IS FALSE OR EVIL. IN THIS WAY OUR INTELLECT IS PERFECTED IN JUDGMENT WHICH GROWS MATURE . . .
>
> — *Rational Psychology* 154

There is no question in my mind that this reflects considerable experience with meditation. It isn't the statement of someone just thinking about the subject. His phrase, "passive potency," is a perfect brief description of the state.

My impression is that Swedenborg began with and used meditation that focuses upon spiritual ideas most of his life. Yet, in the period of *Rational Psychology* and the *Journal of Dreams* he also used meditation as a passive potency, simply watching the internal described above. It would be inappropriate to say he used just meditation. It was part of a whole series of states he explored, all of which tend to make conscious the internal of experience. Minimal breathing and the presence of trance states[8] are signs that he went further than most everyone else

8. Tafel, *Documents II*, pp. 531f.

could do. I would in general say that meditation is a mild, safe and sufficient introduction to these inner states. The advantage over the hypnogogic, trance, and dreams is that there is more consciousness and control. But, on the other hand, the intensity of the inner is in weaker traces than would be true of trance, for instance. But for most people's uses it is sufficient. Swedenborg's experience that these inner states later became more apparent in normal waking life is also the usual experience of those who practice meditation. It isn't that the internal finally finds its way into the external man. It was always there. The person who comes to see the internal begins to recognize it more easily in daily life.

Meditation in Swedenborg's Writings

Meditation in the writings is discussed principally through the terms *meditation* (*meditatio*) and *reflection* (*reflectio*). As used in the writings *meditation* refers to the process itself of seeking inner wisdom while *reflection* is actual perception from that process. Meditation is used both negatively (those given to excess pious meditation may appear sorrowful in the other life, *Heaven and Hell* 360) and positively.

> WHEN A MAN IS IN THE AFFECTION OF UNDERSTANDING, AND THROUGH THIS COMES INTO THE PERCEPTION OF TRUTH, HE IS THEN IN THE THOUGHT OF HIS SPIRIT, WHICH IS MEDITATION; WHICH DOES INDEED FALL INTO THE THOUGHT OF THE BODY, BUT THE TACIT THOUGHT, FOR IT IS ABOVE THIS, AND VIEWS THE THINGS WHICH ARE OF THE THOUGHT FROM THE MEMORY AS BENEATH ITSELF; FOR FROM THESE IT EITHER CONCLUDES OR CONFIRMS. BUT THE AFFECTION OF TRUTH ITSELF IS NOT APPERCEIVED OTHERWISE THAN AS AN EFFORT OF THE WILL FROM SOMETHING PLEASURABLE WHICH IS WITHIN THE MEDITATION AS ITS LIFE. . . .
>
> — *Divine Love and Wisdom* 404

This is a beautiful description of the process. The process is primarily affectional (the affection of understanding) and from this comes perception of truth. This is the thought of the spirit. It is like thought of the body but it is tacit or subtle, as though above and looking down on memory as beneath it. But the affection of truth is barely apperceived as an effort of the will, a pleasure within meditation as its life. And, in another place the writings say that man is aware of meditation but not how the soul produces these things (*Divine Providence* 34). In several ways they reiterate that this is basically an internal affectional process in which man thinks from the affection which is of his love (*Divine Providence* 61). Once the basic process is understood, then it is possible to put the inner focus on spiritual matters. For instance, it is possible to let one's sins come into awareness like a series of memories which spontaneously appear and illustrate a trend like avarice. One can also reflect on ends or uses. In fact meditating on ends is an unusually powerful and life changing approach (*Divine Providence* 152, 296.10). The writings say that the Sabbath day is a day for meditating on salvation and eternal life (*True Christian Religion* 301). Meditation is even a process for communicating with spiritual worlds, for a meditating person may be seen wandering in the society of his own kind (*Heaven and Hell* 438, *Divine Providence* 296.6). In a number of places, the writings indicate that a person's meditation may affect spirits about him. Swedenborg speaks remarkably little of technique but rather describes the inner process, its qualities, and its uses.

The term *reflection* is used in several different senses. The highest and most central of these would be reflection that emerges out of meditation. In this sense it means a spiritual perception of the real truth given by influx from the Divine (*Spiritual Diary* 2221). This is a perception above ordinary thought, a perception of spirit. In a number of instances it is said that spirits don't know their situation unless it is given them to reflect on it (*Arcana Coelestia* 5883). Basically all reflection is from the Divine by influx into man, though it is often perceived as his own (*Arcana Coelestia* 5508). The process in meditation of attempting not to think, and not identifying with thought that emerges, tends to undo proprium and make more apparent reflection which is given, as against reflection as merely a product of one's own thought. For instance, in the example above, when the forceful question came to me regarding what the writings always dealt with, I wasn't aware then that this would answer my question as to the real nature of the New Church. Self-directed thought has a sense of where it is going, whereas this higher thought emerges before there is an understanding of what is being dealt with. It is much more like being given a surprise. It is appropriate that this highest sense of reflection as spiritual truth given to a person should also extend downward and include all perception, even sense perception. After commenting that reflection has more arcana in it than any other matter Swedenborg goes on to say,

> WHAT REFLECTION EFFECTS CAN BE SUFFICIENTLY EVIDENT TO ANYONE, IN THAT HE PERCEIVES NO SENSATION OF HIS BODY OR OF ITS PARTS, NEITHER DOES HE KNOW THAT HE HAS SENSATION, UNLESS HE REFLECTS UPON THAT PART OF HIS BODY; HE THEN PERCEIVES HEAT, COLD, PRESSURE, INDEED HE FEELS THAT WHICH HE FIRST ENDURES.
>
> — *Spiritual Diary* 733

This higher perception of truth or awareness lies behind even ordinary awareness of sensations. The spirit sees through the eye. The spirit makes sight possible. The higher is the cause of the lower. Meditation, by deliberately attempting to become aware of the internal, leads to the perception of influx which is the basis of all life experience. In precisely this way the effort of meditation spiritualizes and turns around the values. Slowly and somewhat laboriously the new student of meditation begins to pick up little fragments of thoughts and perceptions given by influx. Gradually the meditator becomes accustomed to the experience of influx and it becomes apparent in his experience (not just from doctrinal teachings) that all mental life is given by influx. From this view, proprium, what is of one's own alone, looks more and more insubstantial and almost simply a falsity. Spiritual reflection has its own pleasures. An analogy might be of leisurely wandering in a beautiful new garden. Meditation and its companion reflection are acquired tastes. It may seem a mean beginning to spiritual experience to sit and stare at a point, but it takes a great deal to quieten the external mind so that the internal can begin to stand forth. Swedenborg's own concentration was far greater than others will achieve.

Meditation is one of the avenues to regeneration, although this may not be immediately apparent. In the first place it gives voice to the inner, it teaches of influx first hand and thereby helps undo proprium. By opening the internal it opens the way to spiritual perception. Many places in the writings indicate that awareness of the internal or higher is the key to spiritual development.

> THOSE WITH WHOM THE INTERNAL, SPIRITUAL MAN HAS BEEN OPENED INTO HEAVEN TO THE LORD, ARE IN THE LIGHT OF HEAVEN, AND IN ENLIGHTENMENT FROM THE LORD, AND FROM THIS THEY ARE IN INTELLIGENCE AND WISDOM: THEY SEE TRUTH BECAUSE IT IS TRUE, AND PERCEIVE GOOD BECAUSE IT IS GOOD. BUT THOSE WITH WHOM THE INTERNAL, SPIRITUAL MAN HAS BEEN CLOSED, DO NOT KNOW THAT THERE IS AN INTERNAL MAN, STILL LESS WHAT THE INTERNAL MAN IS. . . .
>
> — *New Jerusalem and Its Heavenly Doctrine* 44

Indeed, some will probably respond to this paper by saying it is not possible to become aware of the internal and will cite some passages from the writings that seem to suggest this, e.g. *Arcana Coelestia* 2557. Yet, if these passages are examined they imply that the man who is not spiritual, who is only natural, has a closed internal. These people cannot be aware of the internal. To them it seems merely an unreliable fantasy. The internal can be opened and indeed become very clear and manifest (*Arcana Coelestia* 1175, 1914, 5920). Basically it takes a passive potency, listening and looking, rather than thinking and making. The key to meditation is not the technique, which has been overemphasized by current schools. A sincere fool could succeed with almost any technique. The key is in the quality and persistence of the search, in the person's real ends. No amount of artful mental manipulation will overcome foolish or base ends. All the teachings in the writings about angelic guards on the sacredness of the Word, the angel with a flaming sword, have to do with the guarding of the internal similarly. The student, after making gains in meditation, usually tries to repeat exactly the setting, time, method of concentration, etc., in the hopes of assaulting the internal in the same fruitful way each time. It is a hard lesson to learn that this is simply not possible. The subtlest and most covert maneuvering of the external man simply becomes an obstacle to his own effort. The external's impatience is met by the internal's eternal patience. Let anyone who thinks that any technique opens the internal to his own proprial control try and see how foolish this is. That is part of the heart of the lesson to be learned. Technique has some role, just as I might say one is more likely to have a spiritual experience sitting quietly in church than while arguing with a neighbor. But its role is limited to opening up the first possibility. The root meditative practice is the opposite of mental flightiness and presumption. I hope it is immensely clear that if there is any maneuvering in meditation it is to put down the external man, to make it possible for the internal to be felt, heard and seen. It is precisely because the internal acts so differently—much more clearly, truly and richly—that it begins to educate the dumb external person to the fact that he is dealing with something higher, that is within him and all people. The external must become subject to the internal,[9] which it was made to serve.

Meditation is not for everyone. Some have spent a lifetime in self control. For them a passive potency raises an awesome specter of negative possibilities. I have never known meditation in myself or in hundreds of students that wasn't generally a higher experience than average living. Yet some will construe that a passive potency could leave one open to the forces of hell. We get back so much of what is expected that those with such fears perhaps should avoid the experience unless they work with an experienced teacher. But, for people who would like to experience the internal, it is possible, relatively easy, and rewarding. Personally, I don't see how much of what the writings say of the internal can really be understood until it is experienced. As

9. *Arcana Coelestia*, 5077, 5125, 5128, 5786, 5947, 10272.

the writings imply, there are many more arcana in this relatively simple experience that have not been touched upon here. Our aim was simply to return meditation to some understanding and respectability. For those who wonder what the further arcana could be, they begin with all that the writings have to say of the difference between the internal and external man and lead towards regeneration. In the view of the writings one could not argue that meditation is the only way of regeneration but, because of its direct lessons, it is one of the major ways.

The Psalm of What Is

Hail,
To all peoples,
I have found the Lord
Hidden,
In the most obvious place.

The Lord is
The What Is
That confronts us.
That obvious.

We have intercourse
With the What Is,
And intercourse is the Word,
For it takes place not only in the
  world, in the eyes of others,
But it takes place within,
In the very secret darks
Of what we are.

In here
In what we are
We have intercourse
Man
and I.

Insofar as you love Me
And sum up in your pouch
  All you are,
  All your pride,
  In your little pouch,
  And give this,
Then I answer as the What Is.

Is the answer so obvious
That you do not see
It is the Lord?

For I am the Lord What Is.
It is with Me you have intercourse.
And this intercourse is your life
And Mine
For I too suffer
In the darkness of your soul.
It is that kind of intercourse,
Life and death.

No man —
Sum up what you are
And give it to Me.
You live and breathe and move
In my will.
Your very thinking is My creation
Your very pride is My design,
It is my pleasure of myself
In the creation of what is.

In the secret recesses of yourself
Give me this
And I answer in the most obvious
  way imaginable,
As the what is.
To find me
Give way to what is.
I am not far
To be sought,
Always with you
As I promised,
Constantly by your side,
Falling as you fall,
And rising as you rise
In this what is.

In this pit
My love.
For it is, after all,
Only I.
I make the pit
And the rising and falling
And the trembling you here
And your ability to question me
That lover can say to lover,
In the bed of existence,
Is that you there?

When you are already carried into
  the extreme
Where it can be only I.
And so all of existence
Is our playful, joyous and agonizing
  intercourse,
Where the question of
Is that really you?
Is the issue.

Yet it is only you
and I.
In the whole bed of existence.
And I come to my lover and say,
See,
I made you,
In the bed of existence
You are my substance.
Fear not,
For I am yourself.
Are we not like lovers?

You want to know if it is really me.
And I show you your hands.
I made the whole world.
But, so much of a lover,
I don't mind being your mute hands
In your work.

And yet
I am the What Is.
I am creation
I am all there is,
In endless intercourse
With myself.
The intercourse of the What Is
Is creation.
And were it not for love,
There would be no creation.
Gentle love
Is the root of it all.

All people —
It is I
Who rise and fall with you.
Help Me.
For I am all there is
For I am creation
Your very abode,
Help me
For I live here
With you.

I am, after all,
Both the petitioner
And the petitioned.
Lift Me
  and I lift you

Hurt Me
  and I hurt you.
Yet, I am both of these.

Come,
Your life is intercourse with Me.

Now,
Like gentle lovers
In the bed called world
You
and I . . .
You always have what pleases Me.
. . . .
It is what
You are.